Understanding and Working
with the Spectrum of Autism

also by Wendy Lawson

Life Behind Glass
ISBN 1 85302 911 4
(not available from JKP in Australia or New Zealand)

of related interest

Asperger's Syndrome
A Guide for Parents and Professionals
Tony Attwood
ISBN 1 85302 577 1

Pretending to be Normal
Living with Asperger's Syndrome
Liane Holliday Willey
ISBN 1 85302 749 9

Asperger Syndrome in the Family
Redefining Normal
Liane Holliday Willey
ISBN 1 85302 873 8

Learning to Live with High Functioning Autism
A Parent's Guide for Professionals
Mike Stanton
ISBN 1 85302 915 7

Asperger Syndrome, the Universe and Everything
Kenneth Hall
ISBN 1 85302 930 0

Asperger Syndrome Employment Workbook
An Employment Workbook for Adults with Asperger Syndrome
Roger N Meyer
ISBN 1 85302 796 0

Finding Out About Asperger Syndrome,
High-Functioning Autism and PDD
Gunilla Gerland
ISBN 1 85302 840 1

Autistic Thinking – This is the Title
Peter Vermeulen
ISBN 1 85302 995 5

Understanding and Working with the Spectrum of Autism

An Insider's View

Wendy Lawson

Foreword by Margot Prior

Jessica Kingsley Publishers
London and Philadelphia

First published in the United Kingdom in 2001 by
Jessica Kingsley Publishers Ltd
116 Pentonville Road,
London N1 9JB, England
and
325 Chestnut Street,
Philadelphia, PA 19106, USA

www.jkp.com

Library of Congress Cataloging in Publication Data
A CIP catalog record for this book is available from the Library of Congress

British Library Cataloguing in Publication Data
A CIP catalogue record for this book is available from the British Library

ISBN 1 85302 971 8

Printed and Bound in Great Britain by
Athenaeum Press, Gateshead, Tyne and Wear

The image that comes to me is from shoaling — the very neuro-typical are clumped in the middle of the shoal all facing steadfastly in the same direction at all times; the very autistic are off on their own swimming in every direction without any regard to the shoal; the not so neuro-typical swim in roughly the same direction as the others but on the edge of the shoal, seeing and sometimes going in other directions — varying distances for varying times; the not so autistic may sometimes completely lose sight of the shoal but generally swim within sight of it at a good distance and may sometimes swim along with it from time to time...

If we also assume that what determines the degree of shoaling is not willed — is not within awareness — then we get the initial condition for autism: there are shoaling / flocking equations which predict that the sort of distribution I describe will naturally occur. On the other hand if we bring in awareness it gets complicated, and therefore potentially uncertain and uncomfortable: it becomes choice-laden — but also INTERESTING!! and also with much potential for grouping and subgrouping to relative degrees of flexibility.

But that is just thinking 'aloud'...

Dinah Murray, 2000, from a personal conversation with the author

Acknowledgements

With regards to the writing of this book, there are several individuals that I wish to acknowledge and thank. My life has been made the richer because of their love, acceptance, commitment and trust in me.

- Mick, for all the hours spent helping me to get organised. Such is a consultant's life!
- Vicki, you shared yourself with me and taught me that I am trustworthy, thank you.
- Dinah, special thanks for proof-reading and giving me ideas for this book. To find a 'fellow traveller' of like mind and ideology is such a treasure. I look forward to our continued shared battle for justice!
- So many others of you, who have taken the time to know me or share your story with me, thank you. This book is for you. To all of those I am yet to meet, personally or through this book, I am writing for you.
- Jessica Kingsley and all the team, thank you for believing in me and in the vision of this book.
- Estelle and Barb and John and Debbie, I value your friendship, feedback and support.
- My lovely neighbours, thank you for being just over the fence.
- Don, Alan, Paul and David, my trusty companions in discovery. Where would I have been without you?
- Beatrice, without your tireless commitment to me, and our work, this book would not exist. I appreciate you more than words can say.
- To my Heavenly Father, thank you.

Contents

Appendices

Foreword

The puzzle of autism remains as fascinating today as it was when first recognised more than 50 years ago. We still struggle to understand this disorder and to find ways to connect with people with autism. Wendy Lawson was diagnosed in adulthood with one of the sub-classes of autism, Asperger Syndrome. This is a term which is reserved for people who, despite their autism, are verbally able and not so cut off from the world as are children with more severe handicaps. Wendy is uniquely articulate about her struggles to connect with the world around her, and she is making a wonderful contribution to the understanding of parents, professionals and people with an autism spectrum delay. She does this through her talks and workshops, and her individual interactions with many people.

Now she has provided us with a book which collects together her wisdom and her experience and offers us new insights into under-standing and dealing with this very challenging condition. Wendy has her own language and concepts to help in this understanding. As a way of bridging the gap between people with autism and those without, for example, Wendy explains the differences between what she calls 'neuro-typical' people and those for whom some biological processes have gone awry (autism). She describes autism as character-ised by monotropic thinking or single-channelled views of the world. These are major themes of the book and provide helpful clues to understanding the thinking processes of the person with autism. Wendy reminds us of the traps of assuming that the person with autism understands our everyday language, and she suggests strate-gies for communicating more adaptively. Her aim is to arm parents with knowledge which will help them to relate better to their autistic child.

The book is organised into chapters focusing on different aspects of autism, and each chapter ends with a helpful summary of key concepts. Problems such as anxiety, obsessive behaviours, difficulties with social understanding and communication, and family and sibling issues all receive attention. There is a good summary of cognitive processes in autism achieved through the filter of the author's personal experience.

Throughout the book the themes are focused on practical issues and illustrated with case histories, and sometimes with some of Wendy's own insightful and eloquent poems. The book concludes with 'commonly asked questions about autism' followed by direct suggestions, practical exercises, and strategies which can be helpful for managing difficult behaviours. Despite the fact that we are still searching for the causes of autism, we have made encouraging progress in diagnosis, early intervention, and education for children with this condition. Wendy makes a further contribution to our knowledge which is especially valuable because of its basis in her experience of a life lived with this condition.

This book will speak directly to parents and others wanting to find ways into the world of the person with autism. It is driven by first-hand experience, excellent analytic skills, and substantial experience in sharing knowledge with people working in the field. One of its strengths is its focus on understanding the connections between behavioural problems and inner stress, along with the sensible ideas and recommendations for management of problems.

Wendy is a wonderful builder of bridges between the world of the person with autism and the conventional world. Her book will help many people in both worlds.

Professor Margot Prior
Department of Psychology
Royal Children's Hospital
Melbourne, Victoria, Australia

Introduction

This text is based upon my experience and understanding of autism spectrum disorder (ASD), as well as what the literature says. I was diagnosed with Asperger Syndrome (AS) in August 1994. AS appears to fit at the far end of the spectrum with individuals of mostly average intelligence. According to the *Diagnostic and Statistical Manual of Mental Disorders* (American Psychiatric Association 1994) (DSM–1V), Asperger Syndrome is diagnosed when all the typical signs of autism are present, but the individual has normal language development. However, we do demonstrate the same kind of behaviour patterns as other individuals with autism. For example, we dislike change (we prefer routine); we tend to be obsessive; we become anxious very easily; we take what is said to us literally (for example: train driver says 'Can I see your ticket?' 'No', says the boy. 'It's in my pocket'). The aim of this text is to explore ASD cognitive processes compared with those of the normally developing, or *neuro-typically* developing, population and their effect upon 'stress'. Practical exercises and possible interventions that might aid in stress reduction can be found in Part III.

Overview of autism spectrum disorder

Autism Spectrum Disorder (ASD) is thought to be a neurobiological condition of the brain that impacts upon development (Prior 1992). It may be prompted by one of three general areas: genetic predisposition, brain insult or brain disease (Frith 1992). The spectrum of autistic disorders described in the DSM-IV under the heading of 'Pervasive Developmental Disorders' (I prefer 'delays') is apparently illustrated in individuals who might show poor knowledge of social rules and social skills; exhibit delayed, absent or stereotypical language; have little or no 'theory of mind'; display repetitive and/or compulsive behaviours and are egocentric (Wing 1992). Individuals with autism also demonstrate bizarre responses (resistance to change, peculiar interests, and attachments) and many are echolalic, use idiosyncratic language or pronominal reversal (Gillberg 1991).

ASD relates to a condition that impacts upon a person's ability to understand and interact with the world around them. The latest figures suggest it influences from five to seven children in 1000, (Gillberg 1999) and is found throughout the world (Prior 1998). According to Boyd (1992, p.63), 'autism is one of the most severe childhood disorders characterized by qualitative and quantitative impairments in two way social interaction, communication and a marked restriction in range of interests and activities'. However, I do not experience my being autistic as being 'disordered' or 'impaired', so much as I experience it as being 'dis-abled' in a world that doesn't understand autism!

Although the idea of an autism continuum is popular, for example some researchers believe Kanner's autism (classic autism) and Asperger Syndrome are terms used to describe 'types' of ASD, this is still a topic for debate.

Autism Is

Autism is: being present in this world,
But not entirely of it.
I am one step removed and curled,
The switch just doesn't click.

I perform the role of my perception,
And play many parts so well.
But minus files for my redemption,
My part in life I cannot tell.

Life is like a video,
I watch but cannot partake.
My uneven skills are but an echo,
Of the frustrations which I hate!

However, my focused use of time and space,
I would not give away.
I know that I am especially placed,
For some developed career one day! (Lawson 1998)

Neurotypicality

Neuro-typical, for the purpose of this book, will refer to non-autistic individuals who are of 'normal' intelligence and do not have intellectual, social or communication disabilities. I do understand that this term could be ambiguous and its use serves only to distinguish people who do not have an autism spectrum disorder from those of us who do.

I believe that, as a general rule, misunderstanding between individuals with ASD and individuals with a neuro-typical disposition can be the result of the differing ways we encounter and process life experiences. I will attempt to explore this idea in Chapter 3 by explaining the following concepts that I believe inform my autistic experience and compare them to that of the neuro-typically developing population.

Cognitive processes

In ASD:

- Literality (or taking things literally) (e.g. metaphors, similes, words, expressions)

- Monotropism or being singly channelled (e.g. only able to focus on one thing at any one time, or only comfortable with using one channel)

- Thinking in closed pictures (e.g. not connecting ideas or concepts)

- Non-social priorities (e.g. preferred clothing versus fashion)

- Non-generalised learning (this implies not transferring skills or knowledge)

- Issues with time and motion (this can mean problems with sequencing, timing and/or motor coordination)

- Issues with predicting outcomes (e.g. not learning from experience or being able to forward think and work out conclusions)

- Lacking a 'theory of mind' (not understanding the concept of 'other'; empathy lacks and empathy gaps)

Compare the above with the following that I believe inform neuro-typical experience:

- Non-literality

- Multi-channelling (using several channels simultaneously, e.g. visual, auditory and spatial)

- Thinking in open pictures (this means being able to connect experiences, often visually, in an open and continuous manner)

- Social priorities (e.g. social norms, rules, expectations and being sociable, are seen as a priority)

- Generalised learning (having the ability to transfer skills and knowledge across differing situations)

- Limited issue with time and motion (can appreciate length of time, timing and sequencing; can negotiate stairs, personal space, crowds, and so on)

- Little issue with consequences (able to understand and predict outcomes)

- Possessing a 'theory of mind' (understanding the concept of 'other')

Aims of this book

I suggest that individuals with a diagnosis of autism spectrum disorder (ASD) will utilise distinctive cognitive processes in order to comprehend and make sense of the world around them. This book aims to demonstrate such cognitive processes and help the reader, through reading and written exercises, to comprehend the world of autism and, in doing so, to be able to relate more successfully to individuals with ASD and to their families.

The cognitive processes explored can be compared with those of the neuro-typical world (non-autistic world). This will serve to illustrate the differing ways that individuals with autism inform their experience, compared with those of the normally developing population. For individuals with ASD these differing ways of processing information from their daily experiences may mean the following: using rigid monotropism, which means single channelling (e.g. using a visual channel only to filter information and having a redundant auditory channel); having difficulties with predicting outcomes; possessing a preference for routine; demonstrating obsessiveness; literality; problems with time and motion; issues with non-social priorities; and empathy lacks and empathy gaps (Lawson 1998a; Murray 1992, 1995, 1997).

Neuro-typically developing individuals will not conceive of the world in the same way as those individuals with ASD might. Therefore, the differing cognitive biases for each group will present many difficulties for both individuals with ASD and those interacting with them. Those with ASD may find themselves living in a world dominated by individuals operating from a cognitive mindset quite different to their own. For instance, within the neuro-typical world it is common to be multi-channelled. By this I mean the ability to have multiple interests and be able to focus on more than one thing at one time (e.g. be involved with conversation, listen, think and maintain eye contact at the same time). For many individuals with ASD, however, this would be quite difficult. To engage in conversation alone, would require total focus, and if one had to look at the person whilst engaged in conversation, this could be distracting.

Being usually capable of predicting outcomes and most consequences of chosen behaviour is another facet of neuro-typical development. Adapting to changing situations and circumstances, seasons of the year and other various life experiences, can usually occur without too much difficulty. Neuro-typical individuals may not have huge problems with time and motion (e.g. knowing when they are hungry or full and the right time to eat or stop eating; knowing how to move forward physically and emotionally in time). They are usually understanding and accepting of 'change' (e.g. traffic diversions during road works) and employ social priority (e.g. choosing relationship with another above being alone as a 'norm') (Santrock 1989).

These essential differences in an individual's cognitive make-up could present as a recipe for major difficulties in families with individuals with ASD. These difficulties can attack parental confidence, cause confusion and fear responses in children with ASD and raise stress levels for all concerned. Even with appropriate support, early intervention and the utilisation of full service provision, stress levels for families with a member with ASD (including Asperger Syndrome) appear to be well above those of families with children with different disabilities (e.g. Down syndrome), (Sharpley, Bitsika and Efremidis 1997).

I suggest that attempting to communicate and interact with one another, based upon neuro-typical cognition alone, is like mixing oil with water and creating a cocktail for disaster! However, I also postulate that there is a way for this to change. Just like the agent needed to cause water and oil to mix, there is a recipe that enables mutual understanding of the cognitive processes involved in the ASD condition.

The literature supports the idea that certain cognitive processing talents located within the ASD condition can be recruited and used successfully as a tool for generalising one's learning (Eisenmajer and Prior 1991; Harchik *et al.* 1990; Ozonoff and Miller 1995). If, however, these talents are not understood or explored, then they remain a hidden resource!

This book proposes that although the combinations of multi-channelling, prediction of outcomes, social priorities, non-literality, and 'time coping' contribute towards neuro-typical cognition, this may actually be acting against constructive family relating with individuals with ASD. This being so, the text explores ways of comprehending and addressing this concept.

Sharpley *et al.* (1997) found that a number of factors influenced the well-being of parents of children with ASD. These included the coping and handling of the child with ASD by other family members. For example, the better the coping and understanding ability of other family members, the better the stress levels of parents. They also found a positive correlation between parental confidence and lower stress levels. I believe that parental confidence can greatly increase as the parents understand the cognitive processes of their child with ASD. Then, armed with this understanding and knowledge, the parents would be better able to relate to their child with ASD and orchestrate appropriate behavioural challenges and interventions, both for themselves and for their child.

I believe neuro-typicality can be an impediment to understanding autism and, therefore, it can actually support and increase family stress. This book, however, will enable the reader to discover how the differing perceptions, cognitions, interactions and behaviours of either neuro-typical or autistic worlds impact upon individuals with ASD and their families. It also aims to help readers adjust their understanding and cognitive styles to include that of the autistically developing world.

Asperger Syndrome (AS), so called because Hans Asperger first noted the characteristics of the syndrome in 1944, portrays ASD individuals with normal intelligence as seeming 'odd', egocentric and lacking in common sense. Asperger noted that his subjects seemed socially and physically awkward or clumsy. The autistic traits demonstrated in AS may appear to present in a milder form.

However, I think that when we use the term 'mild' we are in danger of not viewing this disability accurately. For many of us with this diagnosis, we experience our disability in a neuro-typical world as being anything but mild!

I suggest that wherever an individual is 'placed' along the ASD continuum (classic autism, Asperger's autism, pervasive developmental delay, and so on) there are quite specific keys to understanding and effectively interacting with us as individuals. I believe that being ASD may mean the utilisation of specific cognitive processes that enable us as individuals to comprehend and make sense of the world around us. These cognitive processes might be vastly different to those of the neuro-typical world. Why do we avoid eye contact? Why do so many of us insist on routine and sameness? Why do we need to manipulate the world we live in? Why do we fail to generalise our learning? It is hoped that this book will answer some of these questions.

Why write this book?

Autism spectrum disorder (ASD), a term that became popular during the 1990s, is a relatively new concept. The literature appears to support the notion that autism is no longer a rare disorder with clearly defined narrow boundaries but is viewed by many as a continuum (Prior 1998). Bitsika (2000) suggests that in reality, when we look at the autism continuum, we see not one continuum, but three. There is the continuum for high-functioning autism, another for moderate-functioning autism and a third for low-functioning autism. Currently Bitsika makes this statement based upon 15 years of her clinical experience. She suggests that even within the same diagnostic category (high-functioning autism) individuals can present very differently from one another. I find this very interesting, especially as I have noticed this among the neuro-typical population.

Even today ASD is somewhat of an enigma; and with all the expertise of today's minds and revelations, autism is still little understood. One thing that the experts do agree upon is that most types of autism spectrum disorder are probably genetic, involving more than one gene. What triggers this disorder? Well, that's where diversity comes in. There are schools of thought from diet to vaccinations, from vitamin or hormone deficiency to personal choice! We may not know what the trigger is that causes one baby to be non-autistic (neuro-typical) and another autistic. What we do know, however, is that ASD influences the way an individual thinks, feels and experiences life; producing outcomes, for many, that can result in alienation, misunderstanding, depression and even suicide. So, although in the past autism was perceived as being directly related to poor maternal care and attention, today it is considered to be a disorder of the central nervous system (CNS), possibly genetically based (Prior 1992). Children with ASD seem to live in a world of their own and usually resent pressure to be sociable.

This book aims to be one more tool in the pocket of increasing awareness of ASD, its nature, its implications for individuals and their families and possible positive, practical outcomes.

There is much written about biological and psychological bases for autism (e.g. Gillberg and Coleman 1992; Happé 1998), techniques for changing behaviour (e.g. Janzen 1996; Maurice 1996), parenting aids (e.g. Brill 1994; Schopler 1995) and autobiographical accounts of autism (e.g. Blackman 1999: Grandin and Scariano 1986; Lawson 1998b; Williams 1994). However, there appears to be little in the literature concerning the particular understanding of autistic cognition, processing and subsequent behaviours. This text will discuss these issues and, therefore, help the student explore various strategies for further enhanced communication, practical interventions and subsequent positive outcomes.

What this book is not

This book is not about applied behaviour analysis, although such interventions can work well with ASD (see Maurice 1996), nor is it about aiming to make an individual with ASD more socially accept-able and able to 'fit' into their existing environment. Rather, it is about realising the differences between the two worlds of the neuro-typical and autistic experience and, therefore, building a bridge between them, enabling mutual exploration.

Being autistically delayed

Within the world of ASD a diagnosis places the individual upon the autism continuum. This might mean experiencing difficulties with change and preferring routine, tendencies towards being obsessive, being anxious, and taking words and life literally. Difficulties with processing information, non-social priorities and issues with theory of mind type awareness are all consistent with the autistic condition. Being singly channelled (monotropic) and having difficulties with predicting outcomes, are essential components that many of us as individuals with ASD experience (Lawson, 1999a).

According to Tonge, Dissanayake and Brereton (1994) 70 per cent of children with an autism spectrum disorder will also be intel-lectually disabled. This means that their overall intellectual function-ing upon IQ testing falls below a score of 70. IQ tests are assessment tools that enable the administrator to score an individual's intelli-gence quotient (IQ). This is 'a unit for expressing the results of an intelligence test. The IQ is based on the ratio of the individual's mental age (MA) (as determined by the test) to actual or chronological age (CA): IQ = MA/CA x 100' (Kaplan and Saccuzzo 1997, p.643). I have some concerns with IQ testing and ASD, these will be explored later in the text.

It has been said that those who gain a sense of control over their lives and destiny live longer and healthier lives (Bitsika 1999). As an individual with ASD I have noticed that the lack of understanding and, therefore, control over my environmental outcomes, causes me much frustration. In order to cope with this I will often try to manipulate my environment and others who share it with me. This might mean that I need to sit upon a particular seat, eat from a particular plate, or only walk on the outside of someone. I might also insist that other individuals in my life do or say things in a particular way. This appears to be born from a desperate need to regain control and preserve dignity, self-esteem and independence (Bitsika 1999).

The following chapters will take several of the known characteristics of ASD and explore them in detail. As the reader engages in the practical exercises, it is hoped they will be challenged within their own neuro-typical thinking so that their understanding of the world as experienced by individuals with ASD will increase. With this increased knowledge and understanding, practical positive outcomes are able to grow and develop. With this view in mind, unsatisfactory stress levels for individuals with ASD and their families can potentially reduce.

I have stated at times, that normal cognition can act as an impediment to understanding ASD. However, whilst expressing this belief, I think that this needs to be carefully defined. As one authority in the field put it:

> I don't think normal cognition acts as an impediment to understanding autism – if anything it may help. However, the normal affective or emotional functioning of neurotypicals may well impair empathic understanding of autistic functioning. For example, the parent can't easily imagine the autistic person's confusion and stress in social situations because processing social or affective information is natural, unlearned and automatic in neurotypicals. They (neurotypicals) can't perceive that it has to be taught as a cognitive operation for people with autism (L. Bartak, personal communication, 2000).

I understand what is being suggested here. In fact normal cognition suggests that one's intellect should enable a neuro-typical individual to 'learn' to understand autism quite easily, just like one might learn about a new culture or another language!

Perhaps this belief is born from a sense of neuro-typical 'logic', and, in many ways it does make sense. However, if this were the case, if this were the whole story, why do so many neuro-typical individuals have such problems understanding ASD? I would like to suggest it is because ASD cognitive processes are so different, and just using one's intellect to gain understanding of those differences isn't enough. It is also important to appreciate 'why' the differences exist, what they may mean for the individual and their families, and how these differences can be useful in positive practical ways.

Studying the cognitive concepts that apply to ASD and learning them will enable informed communication between us all. This may help to counteract any neuro-typical cognitive and affective patterns of automation that impede understanding. Research has shown that it takes 48 hours to learn a habit, but much longer to 'unlearn' it. Neuro-typicality is what makes a neuro-typical individual neuro-typical! Therefore, even when one understands the concepts and cognitive processes involved with the autistic condition, one will be inclined to revert back towards neuro-typical interpretation of behaviour, just because it is habitual and normal to do so!

Cognition

The following brief outline of cognition is written to help you comprehend both neuro-typical cognitive processes and those of the individual with ASD.

Cognition involves mental operations such as thinking, conceiving, reasoning, symbolising, insight, expectancy, complex rule use, imagery, belief, intention, problem solving, and so forth (Reber 1995, p.133). Cognition suggests that the wheels are turning, and, just like cogs in a machine, these wheels turn cogs that enable other wheels to turn. In other words, there are many facets to cognition. Cognition is a complex arrangement of particular aspects that involve the following:

○ information processing

○ representation and organisation of knowledge

○ complex cognitive skills.

Information processing

Overall, cognition refers to '…all processes by which the sensory input is transformed, reduced, elaborated, stored, recovered, and used' (Neisser 1967, cited in Reed 1996, p.3). We understand cognition to be the acquisition of knowledge; however, this will involve many mental skills. Skills that we probably all utilise will include: pattern recognition, attention, memory, visual imagery, language, problem solving and decision making.

It is these mental operations that are involved with information processing. We take in information via our eyes, ears, mouth, nose and skin. For those of us who are visually able, we receive information from 'seeing'. For those of us who are hearing able, we take note of the sounds we hear. Unless we have a disability or disease affecting our other senses, we also use our senses of taste, smell and touch. When we put all of the information together we have some kind of mental image. This then allows us to form a picture of the information enabling us to decide whether or not we need to retain the information. Will it be useful at some later time? Does it leave us feeling good about something? Is it something trivial or important? Will this picture aid us in our daily life encounters?

If, however, one's senses are not so well coordinated, balanced, definable or separated, then one's processing of information will be different to that of others who use their senses in an integrated manner. One other factor to consider is the length of time in processing information. If information one is receiving needs to be decoded first, then the process will take longer, and the kind of information stored could be influenced by this factor. I suggest to you that this is the case for many of us as individuals with ASD.

Of course, another aspect of information processing refers to the 'schemata' we develop. A schema is simply a template formed from experiences and information, possibly even influenced by one's feelings about the experiences and information. Schemata can be added to and developed over time, as one broadens one's learning and experiences. Templates are just the basic design or outline that one begins with. In neuro-typical development this occurs progressively, over time and in quite a specific order. As children develop they travel through stages of cognitive, physical and moral development. Piaget documented these stages; and, although the literature suggests they may not be as rigid as Piaget originally stated, they do provide a clear framework from which to understand natural development (see Piaget 1954, 1967).

ASD implies pervasive developmental delays. This means that, although children with ASD still travel through the same stages of development, they may be delayed in their starting of a stage and in their completion of a stage. Children and adults with ASD, although of one age physically, may be much younger emotionally. I say this broadly because I believe we 'catch up' over time and the gap between us diminishes with age. Now, if a young person is intellectually disabled, as well as autistically delayed, they will always display limitations due to their disability. However, research has shown that IQ can be improved with learning, practice and repetition of tasks (Lovas 1987). As the saying goes 'use it or lose it'!

Representation and organisation of knowledge

It has been said that we determine what aspects of knowledge we will hold on to, not by aspirations and desire but by the sheer '…qualitative nature of the task and the kind of operations carried out on the items' (Craik and Tulving, cited in Reed 1996, p.147).

Cognitive psychologists tell us that recalling events from memory will depend upon how they have been coded in the representation stage of processing. We are also told that '…the reason rehearsal often results in learning is because people usually attend to the meaning of the material during rehearsal' (Craik and Lockhart, cited in Reed 1996, p.149). However, according to Attwood (1999), individuals with ASD don't read for meaning so much as they read because the words are there! Attwood suggests that when high-functioning individuals with ASD are tested on a reading test, if we have been advised that the test will require us to understand what we read (we will be tested for meaning) then we are able to pass the test. If however, this instruction is omitted, then we may fail the test. What, therefore, does this imply with regard to learning for individuals with ASD?

Happé (1999) and Attwood (1999) suggest that individuals with ASD lack *central coherence*, or the ability to draw all the details together to form a fuller picture. They suggest that it is common for individuals with ASD to attend to detail rather than to the whole picture. This is certainly true for me and plays a part in why my ASD perception can be unlike that of the neuro-typical population.

Attwood (1998) also states that although individuals with ASD have a reputation for their factual and 'long memories', it is more likely that '…they have the inability to forget'. Being able to store facts and factual information does not necessitate one's ability to understand or interact with it. Facts are facts; and although one may learn to introduce them into a conversation at appropriate times, if one is autistic, one may have difficulties when conversing in the social or emotional arena not bound by factual input.

Complex cognitive skills

Cognitive skills will make use of language, comprehension and memory for text, problem solving, expertise, creativity and decision making (Reed 1996). For the neuro-typical population with normal intelligence and minds, these processes enable a developing individual to learn from social interaction, role modelling, personal experience, practice, social norms and expectations. For us individuals with ASD, however, the essential domains outlined above (language, comprehension, problem solving, and so on) are lacking, missing or autistically influenced. The issues of literality in language (non-comprehension of metaphor and simile), subsequent problems with comprehension, reading for meaning, viewpoints on problems and problem solving, issues with empathy and social priorities, all influence how we see and understand the world around us. In other words, when one draws from a different pool, sings a different song, beats a different drum and encounters the realities of life from a different perspective, communication can be difficult.

Having stated these concepts, however, I believe that mutual ground can be found, that bridges of communication can be built, and that the differences that separate the two worlds can become assets that will enrich the lives of those who take the journey.

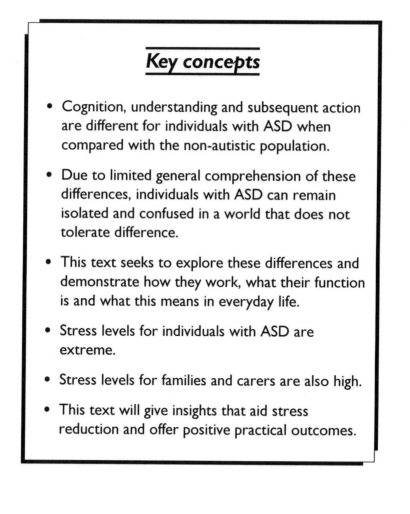

Key concepts

- Cognition, understanding and subsequent action are different for individuals with ASD when compared with the non-autistic population.

- Due to limited general comprehension of these differences, individuals with ASD can remain isolated and confused in a world that does not tolerate difference.

- This text seeks to explore these differences and demonstrate how they work, what their function is and what this means in everyday life.

- Stress levels for individuals with ASD are extreme.

- Stress levels for families and carers are also high.

- This text will give insights that aid stress reduction and offer positive practical outcomes.

PART I

The Spectrum of Autism

General Concepts

CHAPTER I

Keys to Understanding the Spectrum of Autism

I believe the cognitive processes that inform our experience of autistic spectrum disorder are:

- literality

- monotropism, or being singly channelled (serial concepts)

- thinking in closed pictures and non-generalised learning

- non-social priorities

- issues with time and motion

- issues with predicting outcomes

- difficulties with theory of mind (empathy lacks and empathy gaps).

Literality

Individuals with autism, especially children, tend to understand their world in literal terms. This means that we take the spoken word quite literally and respond accordingly. Families with an autistic child, therefore, experience much frustration and may even think that their child is simply out to make life difficult for them!

As people with autism we tend to find our sense of security in our rules, rituals and continuity of roles. These are literally interpreted and carried out 'to the letter'. Therefore, it is very distressing when life does not go according to our expectations. This is one reason why we manipulate our environment and the individuals that share it with us. However, being able to gain the kind of reassurance that we need makes a big difference both to our lives and to the lives of those around us. It is an accepted fact that routines will change and one cannot always maintain sameness. However, one can teach coping strategies that allow for change to occur. Routine and structure are similar but different concepts. As individuals with ASD, we may experience extreme levels of anxiety; therefore, structured strategies to cope with change are essential.

The following examples are of words and situations taken literally:

- Two teenagers yelling at each other. Father comes into the room and yells 'We don't have yelling in this house'. The boys keep yelling.

- Young girl has her Mum's newly baked cake in her hands. Mother says, 'You can't have that'. However, young girl knows that she can because she does have it! Young girl ignores mum and tries to walk away.

- Teacher says to Andrew 'You do know that your homework is due on Tuesday, don't you?' Andrew says 'Yes', but, come Tuesday he does not produce his homework. Teacher only asked if he knew it was due. Teacher did not ask him to give her his homework on Tuesday!

- Mother says to her teenage son 'I'm going out for an hour. Can you tidy your bed?' The youth answers 'Yes, Mum'. When Mum comes home the youth's bed is still 'untidied'. Mum only asked her son if he was *able* to tidy his bed; she did not *tell him* to tidy his bed.

- 'I am bored, can I play a bored game?' 'Of course you can, which board game would you like?' 'I want to play cards.'

- Mother says 'This chicken is tough'. Boy replies 'Does that mean it was difficult to kill?'

- Young man takes too much time to eat breakfast in the morning. Carer complains that because he is so slow, they are often late. However, when they go out for 'fast food', the young man eats his food quickly and attempts to clear the food from other people's tables too! I suggested telling the young man at breakfast time 'this is fast food', might mean he eats his breakfast more quickly!

○ Store detective says 'You can't take those. You haven't paid for them'. Teenager replies 'Of course I haven't, I haven't any money'.

There are many examples of literality in everyday life that pose potential trauma for individuals with ASD. The following two short stories illustrate some common thought processes.

James and the builder

James says to the builder: 'I really am anxious for you to finish off the living room. My parents are coming to visit next week.' The builder replies: 'Yes, I'm able to give you some time to do that. I am off all day on Friday and there will be plenty of time to come over and finish those doors.' However, by 11.00 on Friday morning the builder hasn't arrived. James is pacing up and down the corridor feeling very anxious and upset. He wonders why the builder promised to be at his house all day on Friday. James is unable to concentrate on any of his assignments for university because he is waiting for the builder.

At 12.00 noon, James can wait no longer and he telephones the builder. 'Why aren't you here?' James asks. The builder explains that he has some other jobs to finish, not just the ones for James. He tells James that the doors will only take a couple of hours to finish off and that he will be there after lunch, around 14.00. James puts the phone receiver down and feels a mixture of emotions. He feels silly and very cross. Cross, because the builder didn't explain things to him properly. Silly, because the builder's subsequent explanation made sense! However, unfortunately, he hadn't been able to see that for himself and he now feels very frustrated. He should have been studying but was unable to concentrate because of the confusion and disappointment. Now he has to make up the time he lost.

Tracy goes to camp

The Year 7s had enjoyed their first camp together, and now, as they sat relaxing around the camp fire, Linda, the PE teacher began to play her guitar. Kim produced an enormous bar of Cadbury's chocolate. As it passed between each camper, participants broke off pieces of the chocolate and passed it on. Eventually the decreasing bar of chocolate reached Tracy. Tracy, a 12-year-old with Asperger Syndrome received the chocolate, held it in her hands and looked down at it. There was silence over the rest of the group as they watched Tracy and waited. It seemed like an eternity, but finally Jane broke the silence. 'You can't have the chocolate, Tracy,' she said. Tracy looked up. 'Yes I can!' she exclaimed. Jane reached over to take the chocolate away from Tracy. Tracy jumped up and began to run away.

Half a dozen members of the group chased Tracy for almost 20 minutes around the campfire and the tent site. Eventually, out of breath, Jane called out to Tracy. 'Trace…take a couple of squares from the chocolate bar and please pass it on to Jill.' As the other girls stopped and watched, Tracy stopped running. She bent over the chocolate bar and calmly broke off exactly two squares. She then looked up to locate Jill and moved across to give her the chocolate bar.

Murmuring spread through the group as they returned to their tents. 'Why is Tracy so difficult?' one child grumbled. 'She really pushes her luck,' another muttered. 'I'm glad I'm not one of her friends,' echoed a third.

The above story illustrates so well the issue of literality for Tracy. How can someone tell her that she can't have the chocolate, when she actually does have it? For Tracy, holding on to the chocolate was a time of processing what she needed to do next. Her processing time was interrupted and she 'lost' her train of thought. Without clear instruction and structure to help her, Tracy is in a 'mind field' without a map! However, if Tracy had been given clear instruction about taking two squares from the chocolate bar to have for herself, and then to pass the bar to the camper next to her on her right, this scene might never have occurred.

Tracy has some great qualities. She is loyal, trustworthy, truthful and well committed to doing the tasks she chooses. She would make a good friend. However, because of her literality, as well as having difficulty with her own understanding of everyday issues, she is often misunderstood. This only adds to Tracy's feelings of isolation. She would be a prime candidate for depression, mental illness or even juvenile delinquency.

Monotropism

Having the ability to focus in on one aspect of communication, or upon one interest at one time, has been called monotropism. Rigid monotropism often occurs in my world and I am said to 'have tunnel vision' or to be 'only interested in Wendy's interests'. Monotropism will mean, for many individuals with ASD, difficulties coping with 'change'. For me this is demonstrated in my difficulties with change in routine, expectation, instruction, daily schedule, movement of attention and even incorporating another channel into the present scenario. For example, listening and then being required to participate in decision making (without due time to process information), thus moving from one channel to another.

Monotropism is also evident within the process of interpreting language. For example, when an individual with ASD is told that they are going to grandmother's house, they might be quite upset if that action statement (*going*) is not enacted immediately. *Going* is a verb or 'doing' word. It is totally illogical to be 'going' later or soon. The abstract notions of 'in a while', 'later', 'when we are ready', and so on, do not compute if the term 'going' is used. However, one can prepare to go! Abstract reasoning is quite difficult and many ASD individuals find this very confusing.

According to Murray (1997), the interest systems of individuals with autism, unlike those of the neuro-typical population, tend towards 'attention tunnelling, or monotropism'. Murray states:

> Donna Williams's (1994) analogy for this contrast between herself and ordinary people is that of a busy department store, which in her case can only open one department at a time. To have many interests concurrently active is the norm. This is

called polytropism. Within the neuro typical population poly-tropism is one way of coping with a complex, changing, and only partially predictable environment: it involves spreading the supply of attention thin so as to maintain a degree of generalised readiness. Even the most flexible among us can find this multiply divided attention quite strenuous – we tend to seek recreation in activities which require a relatively narrow focus. (pp. 3–4)

Like Murray I also believe that my discomfort at encountering 'change' is one consequence of my being attention-tunnelled or monotropic.

...it's a lurch for them to be precipitated into a new tunnel. It makes them feel bad. Therefore engaging with them on the basis of their own interests is making it much more comfortable for them than bringing your own pressing interests to bear. In the long run a more accommodating, and more confident, individual may result. (Murray 1996, p.6)

Again according to Murray (1997)

...the integrative function of an interest system must depend very heavily on the individual's capacity to recognise stable structures in their surroundings. For most of us the common culture supplies a huge stock of such structures. But in a relatively monotropic interest system which has achieved minimal connectivity compared with ours, and which has not been open to modification by other people's expectations, then percepts will have much less scope for integration and be commensurately unlikely to make any sense.

At the same time, because of their potential for very narrow focus, percepts which are within an attention tunnel may be particularly vivid and potent while everything outside it is meaningless and dim. Great inconsistency of perception is often reported in autism. People who are concerned with individuals with autism get used to their occasional very emotional out-bursts in response to seemingly minor events. I believe these are a consequence of the great intensity of sensation caused by their superfocussed attention, and the abruptness with which they can experience changes of focus. (Murray 1997, p.8)

Murray (1997) sums this up in her statement: '…percepts in autism will tend to be either extremely vivid or dim and blurry, they will also tend to be isolated, disconnected experiences, not integrated or imbued with meaning from other interests and concerns' (p.9). In Powell and Jordan's (1997) terms, 'the physical properties of objects may be more salient than their functional, emotional or social significance' (p.9). Therefore, according to Walker (1997):

> …the fundamental difference between the autistic and non-autistic condition is at the cognitive level; that non-autistic cognition is a social multi-channel communication system whilst autistic people use only a single channel of communication at any one time… When confronted with the many concurrent facets of communication inherent in the non-autistic social world, without learned coping strategies the single autistic channel is typically and characteristically overwhelmed. (p.6)

In response to perceived 'change' and 'monotropism':

Change

Change, change and more change,
Of context, place and time.
Why is it that Life's transient stage
Plays havoc with my mind?

You said, 'We'll go to McDonald's'
But this was just a thought.
I was set for hours,
But the plan then came to naught.

My tears and confused frustration,
At plans that do not appear,
Are painful beyond recognition,
And push me deeper into fear.

How can life be so determined?
How can change be so complete?
With continuity there is no end,
Security and trust are sweet.

So, who said that change would not hurt me?
Who said my 'being' could not be safe?
Change said, 'You need continuity'
In order to find your place.

For change makes all things different,
They no longer are the same.
What was it that you really meant?
All I feel is the pain.

(Lawson, 1998)

As a way of combating the issue of 'change', many of us as ASD individuals form stringent routines and rules. We aim to organise our lives to follow the same structure every day. Therefore, our everyday lives need to consider a healthy balance of structure, strategy and stress-free states!

Within the education system monotropism is often misunderstood. This may present difficulties at school. The school system is designed for those who can be multi-channelled. Most neuro-typical youngsters enjoy learning a variety of things as well as socialising with their peers. However, when a child with ASD is faced with the school curriculum, has to learn to read, write and socially interact with peers, they may quickly become overloaded and unable to cope. This inability to cope might show itself via their behaviour. They may become agitated, aggressive, frustrated, scared and manipulative. When one understands why a child might be demonstrating inappropriate behaviour, then one is on the right track to amending it.

The following are just a few examples of demonstrated behaviours as a reaction to 'change':

○ *Route changes*. Many children will become upset if a parent drives them to their destination via a different route. They may rock, cover their ears, cry and display strong 'fear' or 'confusion' type responses.

○ *Moving furniture* to a different spot, or changing the bedroom around can cause severe tantrums, rocking, flapping, withdrawal, crying and other distress responses.

- ○ *Tidying toys* or moving something in the child's room can cause distressed responses, as above.

- ○ *Unannounced visitors* or having an unexpected change of routine can cause distressed responses, as above.

- ○ *Changing clothes*, because of seasonal changes, can be very distressing. Being told, 'the sun is out today. You need only wear a T-shirt and shorts' is fine in the warm summer months. What, however, does it mean when the sun is out during the winter months?

One mother reported to me that in a conversation with her teenage son the topic of her being away permanently, as in the event of her death, was mentioned. The child's response was 'who will take me to McDonald's?' When you take life literally, are monotropic and find the concept of 'change' difficult to understand, this response is entirely reasonable.

Thinking in closed pictures

So, we have explored literality and aspects of monotropism. I hope that you are getting the picture. What does it mean to be monotropic and to *think in closed pictures*? As neuro-typical people, you probably think in open pictures. To help explain this concept I often tell the story about the fuzzy felt board at Kindergarten. The fuzzy felt board at Kindergarten has fuzzy felt animals on it. These animals, like goats, cows, sheep and horses, are usually only about 5–10cms in size. I have noticed that the fuzzy felt pig on the fuzzy felt board is usually pink, half the size of my hand and is quite still. However, as a child, when I was taken to visit a hobby farm where I was allowed to get close to and stroke the farm animals, the 'live' pig was not like the fuzzy felt pig on the fuzzy felt board! Therefore, maybe the 'live' hobby farm pig wasn't a pig at all!

My thinking is in closed pictures. The picture of the article, event, experience, and so on, may not take into account intention, context and scale. Due to my being literal, monotropic and experiencing each event as separate and exclusive, I may not link pictures together and inform my experience generally or in an 'open' fashion. This also makes it very difficult to generalise my learnings.

What about generalising our learning? Let me explain why this is so hard for us. Remember that neuro-typical individuals tend to think in open pictures? This means that neuro-typical individuals can add to their learning more easily. They use open pictures to build and integrate their experiences. Piaget (1954) called it *accommodation*. This means one can develop pictures, or schemata and enable learning to generalise to a number of settings. For example, if one eats around a table at home, one might expect to eat around a table in restaurants, and so on. If you think in closed pictures, however, you may eat around a table at home but may not associate eating with sitting around a table outside of home.

As individuals with autism we often need intention, context and scale explained to us. I liked the movie, *The Bone Collector.* There is one scene where the policewoman takes a photograph of a suspect footprint. However, before taking the picture she placed an American banknote next to it, thus giving her the footprint 'size' or context. Using visual supports in education for children with ASD, one needs to make sure that they are accounting for intention, context and scale. It is not helpful to use play plastic zoo animals to prepare children with ASD for a visit to the zoo. How big are the plastic animals?

For many individuals with ASD every situation that we encounter is like encountering it for the first time. We tend not to take what we have learnt from one situation and be able to apply it to another. This makes generalising our learning very difficult. However, many of us can learn to generalise by academically learning the rules for each situation independently (Harchik *et al.* 1990).

Non-social priorities

Most neuro-typical people have social priorities. That is, they prefer the company of others to being alone. Their decisions encompass the wants, needs and opinions of others. What would it be like, however, if you were not aware of 'other'? If empathy was foreign to you or the concept that others were different to you wasn't part of your understanding? There was a time when I didn't talk. Not because I couldn't, but I thought everyone knew what I wanted already, there was no need to tell them. I was unaware that others were separate from me. I needed to learn this. I still have non-social priorities, but I have learnt that others have different views to mine. I need to consider them in relation to myself. I'm still working on this realisation!

My life and yours

'Wendy, Wendy' I hear the teacher say.
'Wendy, Wendy, please look this way'.
'Wendy, Wendy', I hear the children say.
'Wendy, Wendy, please come and play'.

I hear the words that come each day,
'What do they mean?' I hear me say.
Words without pictures simply go away.
I turn my head and look instead
at all that glitters; blue, green and red.

'You'll like it here' Father speaks,
Come and play with Billy'.
Inside my head my brain just freaks,
'How can they be so silly'?

'Why would I want to do this thing?'
My mind can find no reason.
'Please leave me with the sparkly string,
This gives me such a feeling.'

(Lawson 1999)

'Wendy appears to be almost incapable of doing as she is told,' my school report said, and then went on, '…she must learn to have the right thing at the right time e.g. "a pen".' 'Wendy must GROW UP!' These words are taken from my Year 7 school report (see Appendix 5). I wish sometimes, that one could just 'grow up'. I'm assured, however, that this takes time! I spent many years on medication. This may have curbed my anxiety and slowed me down somewhat. What it didn't do was explain social interaction, the 'usual' rules of what it means to be human.

Issues with time and motion

'Time; the present, past or future appear to possess a constant sameness' (Lawson 1997, p.5). Sometimes events that are stored in my long-term memory (and this is probably so for others with ASD) present not as parts of the past but as very present issues. Time, therefore, appears to always be in the present.

What is time?

> I tried to climb the big oak tree
> Scampered across and scraped my knee.
> I walked for hours, picked some flowers.
> If only I could just be me!
>
> I watched the boy who lived next door.
> He had a kite, I watched it soar
> He had a bike, the boy next door
> He had a car, I heard it roar.
>
> The boy next door then moved away,
> So did his kite and bike and car, they say.
> I watched and listened, just in case
> But they were gone and in their place
> The boy next door just was no more.
>
> So did they really exist, or were they just a dream?
> How can they be there and then be not?
> Is it like something that I forgot?

(Lawson 1999)

Concepts of 'the future' are very difficult to imagine. Other people, events and happenings may move on, but for me and some other individuals with ASD they are left behind. My emotions, feelings, thoughts all stay fluid, but they don't seem to move on when time changes. Of course, some aspects of time do move forward. People may notice that they are ageing, but for myself and many other individuals with ASD, even this may take time to notice!

The irony of this aspect of ASD is demonstrated in my life constantly. Even though my mind can hold on to many amazing facts and facets of knowledge, I have an array of learning difficulties and can be very forgetful. For example, sometimes I may forget what I need to buy at the shop, but I can't forget the theme of a video, the outfit someone was wearing, or the layout of a venue I visited.

All is calm, all is tonight...

The cold damp air rushes past me. The church bells are getting louder now, more insistent, threatening 'hurry up, hurry up'. The hour strikes six o'clock and I just make it through the door as the last dong of the big bell sounds out.

Inside, all is quiet and very dimly lit. Amongst 70 or so people about eight candles give out the only light. There is no sound here. The sweat runs down my back as a response is squeezed out of my body. The cold to the warm breeds discomfort – no matter, I will soon adjust. But, how long is 'soon'?

The priest begins with his chant in Latin and the heads in front of me respond with equal ambiguity. I linger, not understanding the foreign words whispered around me, but trying to 'get into the 'spirit' of things. Alas, I fail! 'How long will this take?' 'Can I go now?' 'No, Wendy, it is not yet time.' 'When will it be time?' I ask in my usual tone of voice. 'Ssshhh' comes the reply. Finally, the service comes to a close and the masses file out into the community hall for breakfast.

Down here the candles glow brighter and the nameless faces form smiles. The lights bounce and shimmer in the children's eyes and the grown-ups stir the silence with loud laughter. Much conversation emerges and the older folk of the village talk of 'long ago' and 'when I was a child'.

> Coffee is passed around as the white bread is buttered and spoonfuls of jam are dolloped onto small plates. In between the various stories, small children giggle and teenagers blush – the men share achievements and losses as the winter rains continue down the battened glass panes of the church hall.

> Inside my heart a door opens. Somewhere, in the days of yesterday, a memory is brought forth for today. It is good to be here. For a few moments, maybe even a season, my own dragon is subdued. 'Is it time yet?'
>
> (Lawson 1997).

Not moving forward in time

'Johnny, why did you trip Ben over? He didn't do anything to you!' the teacher asked. 'He was wearing that yellow coat he wore last year, when he tripped me up,' replied Johnny.

As stated previously I believe that most individuals with ASD are monotropic (Lawson 1999a; Murray 1992, 1995, 1996). This implies only being able to focus on one thing at one time. Having a monotropic disposition would certainly make generalising one's experience and understanding quite difficult. This could also have an impact upon the understanding of time. The knowledge of how long something lasts (e.g. a moment; a few minutes; an hour, etc.) can initially be learnt, by many within the neuro-typical population, as one comprehends the length of a day and night, minutes and seconds, or learns to tell the time by reading a watch or clock. Eventually, as one gets older, one appears to have almost an instinctive ability to 'read' one's inner clock of whether or not an hour has passed, or just a few minutes. This process, however, seems to elude me and many other ASD individuals. To imagine what it might be like for us, maybe neuro-typical individuals could think of themselves at times of utter focused single attention, they might be quite surprised at how much time has gone past without their noticing it!

The latter can be the experience for many individuals with ASD. Being singly channelled, placing all our energy and thinking into doing one thing at one time, can mean missing the cues that time can offer. For some of us this may mean not noticing when we are hungry or tired, need to go to the toilet, or are in pain. For others this may mean difficulties with moving on emotionally.

Close your eyes for a moment. Imagine yourself lost in a desert without signposts. How can you know the right way to turn? What might you be feeling? How would you decide what to do? This is what it might feel like for an ASD child at school, or the teenager in the cloakroom, or the young adult starting work. Whatever *is* it that allows neuro-typical individuals to know how long the gap is during conversation, or when it's the other person's turn to speak? How can you know that it's time to let go of that hurt from the past? Where does the idea, that 'it's time to stop now' come from? Whatever it is that neuro-typical individuals possess that gives them a sense of 'timing', we, as individuals with ASD certainly lack it. Timing is everything. So what do you do when you don't have it? Well, you use other means to stay in control. You use routine, ritual and repetitive behaviours. If there are no rules then you invent them. There have to be guidelines. How else will you know what to do?

The following stories will help to demonstrate ASD difficulties with 'timing'.

Breakfast time

> *Ann*: Wendy…why do you always leave the lecture before it's finished?

> *Wendy*: Oh, I usually get hungry at 10.30 so I need to go to the café and buy a doughnut and a coffee.

> *Ann*: But, why not have a good breakfast before you come to Uni and then you could stay until the lecture finishes before going out to morning tea at 11.00?

> *Wendy*: Well, I'd like to, but I always miss breakfast time.

> *Ann*: Why do you miss breakfast time?

> *Wendy*: I'm usually on my computer at breakfast time, and then breakfast time finishes. So, I come to Uni and get hungry at 10.30.

> *Ann*: When is breakfast time?

Wendy: Oh, everyone knows that breakfast time is between 7.00 and 7.30am.

Ann: But Uni doesn't start until 9.30, you have plenty of time for breakfast!

Wendy: No, I don't. I miss breakfast time.

Ann looks at Wendy and then makes a suggestion.

Ann: Wendy, what if you were to think of this differently? What if breakfast time wasn't just between 7.00 and 7.30am. What if it were 'time for breakfast' any time you liked?

Wendy thought about this for a moment. Then the girls explored the idea some more. Finally, Wendy agreed that this was a good way to think about breakfast. Instead of it being 'breakfast time', which is set and unchanging, it could be 'time for breakfast'. This could be any time you liked! Why, one could even have cornflakes at midnight if one wanted to!

The washing

Sharon sat in the kitchen looking out of the window. In one corner of the room the wet washing lay in the blue plastic clothes basket. The sky looked cloudy. 'Would it rain?' thought Sharon. 'It looked like rain yesterday, but the clouds remained un-opened', her thoughts continued. It had been the same situation all week. The now partly damp washing was still in the basket. The dirty linen basket was full, so it too demanded to be washed! Sharon had been sitting in the kitchen all morning. It was the same yesterday. It was just too difficult to make a decision. She needed to know what to do. But even organising to contact someone to ask their advice, seemed beyond her. Sharon continued to sit in the kitchen.

Taking too long in the shower

John was in the shower. 'Come on John, you're taking too long in the shower. There won't be any hot water left for anyone else!' said Paul. John always took his time to get ready in the mornings, and quite often the rest of the household suffered too. 'Oh John, come on, we'll all be late now', said Jane.

Paul came to the autism workshop. 'How can I organise John so that he doesn't take too long in the shower?' he asked. Paul and the workshop facilitator [Wendy Lawson] talked together at some length. It was agreed. John took words literally. Telling him not to 'take too long' in the shower, was as meaningless as saying 'how long is a piece of string?' Instead, it was suggested that Paul devise a way of letting John know the timing of each showering preparation and activity.

SOLUTION TO TAKING TOO LONG IN THE SHOWER

A short story was prepared as an instructive outline detailing the procedure. John likes *The Simpsons*, so we used a comic strip story about Homer Simpson having his shower and then suggested John do the same as Homer does in the story. For example: 'Once inside the bathroom, John, take off your nightclothes and place them on to the chair. Next, turn on the taps, make sure the water is a nice warm temperature and not too hot or too cold. Step into the shower. Pick up the soap and rub it over your body. You can count to 60 whilst you place the sponge with the soapy water on it all over you. Firstly, wash as far down as possible (from your face, neck, shoulders, arms, etc). Then wash as far up as possible (toes, feet, legs and thighs). Then wash possible (between the tops of your legs and all around). By the time you reach 60 you will have washed all of yourself, except your hair.'

Sometimes Homer or John will wash their hair also. So, counting to 60 again, John puts his head under the water spray and gets his hair wet. Then John picks up the shampoo container, squeezes about a spoonful of shampoo on to his hands and rubs this into his hair. Now, as John counts down from 60 to 1, he washes all the shampoo and soap off from his body. When John gets to number 1, the soapiness is gone from his body and he turns off the taps. Now John steps out of the shower, picks up the towel and dries himself. When John is dry he can come out of the bathroom with his towel tucked in around his waist.

To help John with his showering timing, Paul was to knock upon the bathroom door. One knock was to advise John it was time to use the soap. Two knocks meant it was time to turn taps off and dry himself. Three knocks meant it was time to put the towel around himself and exit the bathroom.

Two weeks after Paul began to use this technique I received a phone call. 'Wendy,' said Paul, 'it works!' John was taking, on average, only ten minutes to have his shower. He was a much happier teenager, and the rest of the household were happier too!

Issues with predicting outcomes

I suggest that life for me as an individual with ASD needs to be structured and orchestrated. This is helpful to me due to my difficulty with predicting outcomes. For example, a child's need to line up objects or engage in other ordered tasks and obsessions is born from the need to know what will come next and to be sure that this will always happen. Perhaps the reader could pause for a moment and imagine how life might be if they were not able to predict consequences!

When my young son Tim, a lad with Asperger Syndrome, was twelve, a policeman told us that Tim had been down at our local railway station with some bigger lads, throwing rocks at the passing train. Upon questioning, Tim, however, was emphatic that he hadn't thrown rocks, they were stones, and that he hadn't done anything wrong because he had thrown them *over* the train, not *at* the train! This inability to predict an outcome or fully understand consequences can be a strong component of the ASD personality. It would be fair to say that due to being literal, monotropic, a processor of thoughts as closed pictures, and someone who has problems forming consequences, individuals with ASD may not 'see' the reasoning or rationalisation of events the same way as that of the neuro-typical population. We also may not take the learning of one event and apply its 'wisdom' to another situation.

Egocentricity, eccentricity, and emotional immaturity make up a lot of who I am. I seem to be a bundle of uneven skills. I have university qualifications, I have been married, and I have four grown children. However, I have huge problems with being disorganised, getting lost, using public transport, understanding others, and just the practical interactions of social situations. I think many of you might be saying 'So what, I do as well.' I know that neuro-typical individuals might have issues in these areas but I would suggest to you that it is the degree of the 'issue' that separates us. How many of you need to sit down on the path outside of a supermarket and do breathing exercises because someone changed the tinned soup aisle?

Difficulties with theory of mind

Sometimes inappropriately called 'mind reading', theory of mind refers to the ability to comprehend the fact that 'others' have their own thoughts, emotions and opinions which may be different from one's own. Sometimes it is referred to as having the ability 'to put oneself in another's shoes' or 'to see things from another's perspective'.

Recently I was at a very large conference. One of the activities at this conference centred around the release of a song supplied to customers via a CD-Rom. The theme and title of this song was 'Mind blind'. As I sat and listened to the words of this song a wave of sadness and frustration swept over me. 'If people think I am "mind-blind" because of my autism, then it implies that they are "mind sighted".' In my studies of neuro-typical individuals I have not found this to be the case! I don't think that individuals read one another's minds at all. I think that, if they are interested, they will attempt to put a picture together that attempts to inform them of the person's mood, intention, character and probable action. I understand that neuro-typical individuals do this by reading verbal expression, body language, context and expectation. Due to my being autistic, however, I may need to use other skills to help me comprehend or 'read' others. This will probably take me longer, and I may not be so accurate as a neuro-typical individual, but, I am not 'mind blind' any more than men are 'mind blind' when it comes to understanding women! We are just 'different'.

In fact, research conducted by Grossman *et al.* (2000) suggests: 'Individuals with Asperger Syndrome may be utilizing compensatory strategies, such as verbal mediation, to process facial expressions of emotion...' (p.369). This means we use different 'clues' to enable us to 'read' others. We often need to listen rather than look. The words people use, are often the key for us to enable understanding. If people do not use clear language, then I can find it hard to work out what they mean.

The ability to understand that other people have their own thoughts and beliefs, quite separate from one's own, is a neuro-typical development. By the time a child is three or four years old, many can appreciate second-order beliefs, for example, 'he thinks that she thinks' (Sullivan, Zaitchik and Tager-Flusberg 1994). How-ever, this may not be the case for individuals with ASD. The inability to 'put ourselves in another's shoes' (i.e. we are only able to view life from our own experience and unable to appreciate how someone else might experience life), can be quite central to my being autistic. For this reason I and many other individuals with ASD are seen to be egocentric and may even appear selfish.

In many ways being selfish concerns an ability to choose 'self' over 'other'. For individuals with ASD, however, being only aware of 'self' is not so much of a choice as a predetermined existence. Bio-logically, this is one of the outcomes of the way my ASD mind is organised. Having the cognitive disposition to comprehend the idea of 'other' is either missing altogether, or is limited (Baron-Cohen 1989; Baron-Cohen et al. 1997; Baron-Cohen, Leslie and Frith 1985). However, it certainly can be developed with time and effort!

Practically, this poses a range of problems for a socially minded neuro-typical world, as well as for individuals with ASD having to live here! For instance, mutual human interaction tends to demand emotional and cognitive understanding as a matter of 'right'. It views intolerance and indifference towards others as undesirable and 'bad'. Therefore, when one encounters a self-centred individual in the classroom, schoolyard or work place, one forms a judgment about them. Moving along in one's thinking, self-centred can become 'selfish', demanding, mean, not useful, non-productive and not worth investing in. For individuals with ASD, this is a dilemma! However, when we view someone as being eccentric and egocentric, we tend to think 'artist, savant, genius, musician, mathematician, professor...' We see 'focus' in such people and even forgive their inability to be sensitive to the needs or opinions of others. So, how about we change our thinking from 'selfish' to 'focused'?

Within the autistic spectrum the ability to have a 'theory of mind' varies from nonexistent to being there, but in a limited fashion. This most important ability, however, can become a learned skill for some (Ozonoff and Miller 1995). Being taught the social skills of sharing, listening, being polite, being considerate and affording to others the right to be different, are abilities that enable individuals with ASD to partake in corporate life. Supporting the cognitive awareness of 'other' and teaching 'theory of mind' is also available to many individuals along the spectrum (Eisenmajer and Prior 1991).

How does having difficulties with 'theory of mind' impact upon individuals with ASD? The following examples and stories demonstrate some of the practical problems that we can experience.

- When a school event has been organised and then fails to happen as timetabled, planned or expected an individual with ASD might believe that the organiser is incompetent, mean, not very intelligent, or should simply give their job to someone else who will do it efficiently! *The thought that plans can change for a variety of reasons is not automatically processed.*

- A child with ASD may be fascinated by any number of interesting encounters, but may fail to recognise the effect of such endeavours. For example: David is fascinated with the knowledge that tears come from tear ducts and when crying begins the tear ducts open and water runs down one's face. David will initiate this experience by poking the eyes of young children or animals, with his finger or with a stick. When he succeeds in making the tears appear, David is overjoyed! *The thought that he is hurting someone else and that this in not appropriate, is not automatically processed.*

- Amy loves to eat McDonald's hot chips. When taken to the fast food outlet, Amy does not restrict her eating of chips to her own portion. Amy will endeavour to eat any other child's lunch as well as her own. *The concept of 'ownership', this is mine and that is yours, is not automatically processed.*

- A newly married couple, of whom one partner has a diagnosis of ASD, are coming to the end of an evening of television.

The wife says 'Darling, I'm going to bed now'. The husband says 'Goodnight'. The wife replies 'Aren't you coming too?' To which the husband retorts 'You're a big girl now, surely you can go to bed by yourself!' *The thought that his wife wants him to come to bed because she wants to cuddle up with him and enjoy his being with her, is not automatically processed.*

In order for the processes of 'theory of mind' to occur, however, one needs first to understand its absence. If the idea that others are separate from self, have their own thoughts and feelings and may not operate from monotropic interests, is not comprehended, why do we judge behaviour as if it were?

What might it mean when a plan or expectation is not fulfilled?

When individuals have a good understanding of 'other', it might mean that they can cope with change quite well too. They can utilise their 'other' skills to work out an alternative action or solution to a problem. They will be able to predict what an individual might do, think or choose, if not always accurately! This is a coping strategy that compensates for when changes occur that are outside one's control. This skill is quite difficult for me and for many other individuals with ASD. We need strategies instead!

Preparing for anticipated or expected change will mean that one has time to devote to the necessary issues. Remembering that although time is a positive factor, too much time or advance warning may create unnecessary anxiety. Sometimes only a day's notice is necessary, sometimes a week or just a few seconds. How much notice of change needs to be given will depend upon the individual's personality, needs and adjustment factor towards change in their environment.

When an individual is non-verbal, visual supports are very important. Showing photographs of intended change, sequencing events, unfolding stages, and so on, are vital to gaining an appreciation of what is to come. Even children with language skills may benefit from photos or visual attempts to show expected change. For the older individual, cartoons or comic strip stories can be useful tools to demonstrate anticipated changes.

For unexpected change, when there is no time for preparation, thinking ahead can be useful. For example, just as one might carry candy or a puzzle book in one's bag for a neuro-typical child in case of emergencies, one can be equally prepared for unexpected change for individuals with ASD. For example, for my son Tim, having a particular game at hand, (e.g. Game Boy or some other electronic game, that is only introduced as the 'unexpected event game' for times of unanticipated change) proved to be quite useful.

Be careful not to use neuro-typical assumptions

A young Mum says to me 'My ten-year-old autistic son is so jealous of his baby sister, I can't leave him alone with her. He tries to hurt her at every opportunity and I'm not coping with his behaviour.' With her words in mind do I conclude that her son is jealous or might there be something else happening? Ask yourself the question 'Is jealousy born from a knowledge of how others impact upon us, or is it not?' If your answer is 'yes', 'probably' or 'I think so', then maybe this lad isn't jealous at all! Maybe he enjoys the spectacle of the baby's contorted expression as she cries? Maybe he enjoys the response he receives from his parents when he hurts the baby? Maybe he doesn't understand the interaction from the baby's perspective? Has he any concepts to build an understanding that his hurting the baby is uncomfortable for her, is undesirable and is not appropriate? If the latter is a consideration then by giving the boy attention (as one might in the case of jealousy) one might actually be increasing the boy's potential to do harm to the baby. Rather than relieving the cause of the boy's behaviour, one might be adding to it!

It might be more useful to teach the boy how to be appropriate. If one were to buy a throw away (disposable) camera and take a picture of the child as he was about to 'poke' the baby, this could be used as a tool to educate. When you have developed your picture it needs to be given a Velcro backing. You can make a board for the picture to be placed upon and you can have red markers that you can use to put a big red cross over the picture. This indicates 'No, hurting the baby.'

Your next photo can be of the child with his arm gently around the baby. With your red marker you can place a red 'tick' over the picture. This says 'Yes, loving the baby.' When the boy chooses to 'be nice' to the baby he should be suitably rewarded. The reward should motivate him and give him more pleasure than the 'show' from a tormented baby and her parents!

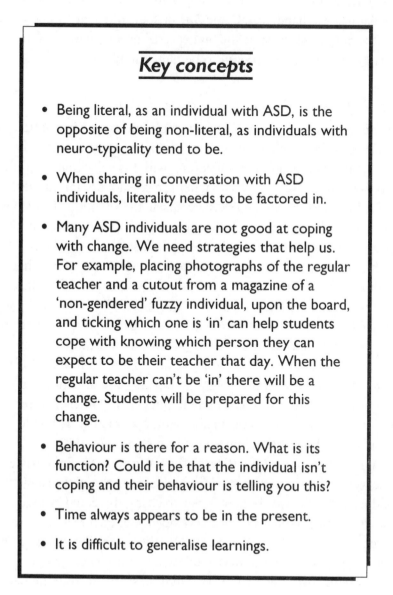

Key concepts

- Being literal, as an individual with ASD, is the opposite of being non-literal, as individuals with neuro-typicality tend to be.

- When sharing in conversation with ASD individuals, literality needs to be factored in.

- Many ASD individuals are not good at coping with change. We need strategies that help us. For example, placing photographs of the regular teacher and a cutout from a magazine of a 'non-gendered' fuzzy individual, upon the board, and ticking which one is 'in' can help students cope with knowing which person they can expect to be their teacher that day. When the regular teacher can't be 'in' there will be a change. Students will be prepared for this change.

- Behaviour is there for a reason. What is its function? Could it be that the individual isn't coping and their behaviour is telling you this?

- Time always appears to be in the present.

- It is difficult to generalise learnings.

- Physical movement through time or the timing of movement, is not automatically processed.

- Monotropism means only using one channel at one time. This is great for being able to stay focused. It is not so good, however, if that one channel is interrupted by another telling you to use some other channel. For example: an individual is using the tactile channel of 'touch' to navigate through the process of getting dressed. 'Look at what you are doing' someone shouts! Individual loses track of what they were doing, gives up and gazes into space.

- We often need some form of prompting to move us through or along the process of a 'timed' event. For example, counting numbers through the process of showering.

- To have a 'theory of mind' does not mean that one can read the minds of others!

- To be 'mind-blind' is not an autistic phenomenon so much as a state of being that all humans can experience at some point or another.

- The best ways to communicate are to be sure that we are each saying and hearing the same thing.

- I need people to use clear language so that I can understand what they mean.

- I need a 'strategy' that will help me to cope with change. I cannot automatically process life events.

Points to ponder

- ◦ Although it is not common practice for neuro-typical children to use one favoured interest across their school curriculum, it can be a most useful motivator for children with ASD.

- ◦ Helping ASD individuals to understand their own literality and teaching them how to check out the words and meanings of others' conversations would be a very useful strategy. This could help to lower frustration levels and build self-esteem.

- ◦ Although having the ability to comprehend the mind-set of another may not be a naturally acquired outcome for individuals with ASD, it can be learned!

CHAPTER 2

Differences in 'Labels' Along the Autism Continuum

Key terms in autism

- ○ pervasive developmental disorder (PDD)

- ○ autistim spectrum disorder (ASD)

- ○ pervasive development disorder not otherwise specified (PDD-NOS)

- ○ Asperger Syndrome (AS)

- ○ classic autism (Kanner's Autism)

- ○ high-functioning autism

Many times the question has been posed 'What are the differences between Kanner's autism and Asperger's autism?' If one refers to the DSM–1V it seems that it might be a matter of language development. For example, individuals diagnosed with Asperger Syndrome should have normal language development. Whereas individuals diagnosed with classic autism might have delayed language development or be non-verbal. But is it quite that simple? What is normal language development? Does it differ from family to family? I have a diagnosis of Asperger Syndrome, but I didn't talk until I was four years old. Is this normal language development? I think in rhyme, most of the time. Is this usual? My speech tends to be pedantic, long-winded, slightly 'old-fashioned' and often inappropriate. The research is showing that it's not so simple (Rickarby, Carruthers and Mitchell

1991; Tantam 1988; Tantam, Holmes and Cordess 1993; Wing 1981).

Try a simple test. Take the following characteristics list, associated with ASD, and locate which characteristics you believe belong to which diagnostic label – classic autism, Asperger Syndrome, high-funding autism, PDD-NOS.

- ◦ Dexterity
- ◦ Clumsiness
- ◦ Intellectual ability
- ◦ Disability
- ◦ Uneven skills distribution
- ◦ Social awkwardness
- ◦ Literality
- ◦ Eccentricity
- ◦ Egocentrism
- ◦ Splinter skills
- ◦ Language problems
- ◦ Communication issues
- ◦ Inability to generalise particular learnings
- ◦ Thinking in pictures

Many researchers today believe Asperger Syndrome and classic autism may be more alike, than they are different. According to Rickarby *et al.* (1991), 'a higher level child with autism, while highly distinct from an Asperger Syndrome child at 4, may be similar at 14' (p.341). Looking back over my life I think this would be true for me. If, in fact, the difficulties remain extensively of the same nature, whichever diagnosis a child with ASD receives, then surely each and every individual, wherever they are on the continuum, will need support and encouragement.

One family's story

Tom is a fifteen-year-old teenager who was diagnosed as having ASD when he was thirteen years old. Tom is third generation Australian and there is a history of learning difficulties in both his paternal and maternal family. After repeated concerns over Tom's behaviour (he seemed antisocial and was finding it hard at school) Tom's parents consulted with a multidisciplinary team at a major hospital near their home in Australia.

Tom has an IQ within the normal range and attends the local secondary college. Due to the fact that Tom is not intellectually disabled and he is not considered either a danger to himself or to others, he does not fulfil the criteria for an aide at school. However, Tom is part of an integration programme, which has been developed for him, and his teachers are aware of his disability.

Tom has a sister (Sue) who is two years younger than him, and Tom's mother reports that the two children get along relatively well. Tom's mother (Sharon) and father (John) both have careers. Sharon is a local primary school teacher and John is a bank manager. John is able to take Tom to school in the morning on his way to work and Sharon brings Tom home. Sharon is more available to Tom because her working hours allow her to spend more time at home. However, John supports both of the children in their recreational activities, his daughter Sue loves netball and horse riding, while Tom enjoys computer games, chess, basketball and walking.

Tom is usually a very happy and amiable young man but like most individuals with an autism spectrum disorder, he dislikes change. Therefore, in order to avoid the fear and confusion of change Tom has developed certain routines, rituals and coping strategies. For Tom, it appears that maintaining routine and structure are consistent needs that dictate his sense of well-being and motivation. Consequently, Tom can respond to perceived change with outbursts of aggression.

Some of Tom's routines and rituals generally do not interfere with daily functioning. For example, Tom always wakes up at seven in the morning and goes to bed at ten in the evening. He eats only toast for breakfast and insists on three sugars in his tea. However, other compulsive desires can cause problems with social interaction. For example, Tom obsessively smells everything, even when it happens to be the perfume on a stranger in the supermarket!

Tom would like to have a friend with whom to share his interest in chess. Unfortunately, Tom does not make friends easily, and when he does they usually do not remain friendly for long. This seems to happen because Tom does not appreciate the social cues of normal interaction. Therefore, Tom appears self-centred and egocentric. According to Sharon, Tom's associates view Tom as being odd and poor company.

Frith (1992) suggests that persons with ASD do not appear to be 'socially tuned'. That is they lack the theory of mind that enables them to comprehend how another person is feeling. Frith, also states that some persons with ASD have 'all the trappings of socially adapted behaviour' but that this is learned behaviour that only resembles normal functioning and is born from 'abnormal functioning processes'.

Another challenge that faces Tom is his literal translation of language. 'Literal use of language is an important feature of autistic communication' (Happé 1991 cited in Frith 1992). It would appear that just as Tom perceives his need for structure and routine, literality correlates with Tom's stage of cognitive development. According to Tonge et al. (1994), such communication difficulties and aberrant cognitive skills are central to the autistic condition. However there is much debate as to why this is so.

Autism, as described by Kanner (1943) and as further outlined in the DSM-IV, is diagnosed in children as young as two years of age. However, although Tom has had challenging behaviour and stereotyped interests as far back as his mother can remember (e.g. he only lined up his toy cars, never played normally) he did not receive a diagnosis of classic autism. Tom was diagnosed with Asperger Syndrome at the age of nine. This was probably because Tom does not have an intellectual disability and he developed normally. That is, he walked, talked and progressed through childhood developmental milestones as any other child. In fact, at kindergarten Tom seemed particularly bright and capable.

The fact that Tom did not play with his peers but preferred to line up his toy motor cars and place them in order, according to their colour, was seen simply, by his teachers, as being idiosyncratic to Tom! Tom also has good verbal skills and this masked other problems that he had with interpretation. His primary school teacher reported that Tom seemed 'selective' in his hearing. He only responded to instruction when he wanted to! However, according to Tantam *et al.* (1993) it is more likely that Tom did not respond because he did not understand what was being asked of him. This may be partly due to poor eye contact and, therefore, poor interpretation of expectations. Bartak (1994) suggests that due to good verbal skills individuals with Asperger Syndrome may not be diagnosed early 'because they have unimpaired speech'. In fact their language skills most likely mask the true picture of their problems.

Tom's strengths:

- *Behavioural*: Tom is consistent and loyal. His single-mindedness is endearing and it is easy to relate to him on matters of mutual interest. When Tom is interested in a topic he stays focused, and this can be a useful aid in Tom's learning process.

- *Communicative*: Communication for Tom is often best when it is on his terms. This means that when engaged in conversation Tom prefers to talk about the things that interest him. This can be a useful strategy that enables the other party to comprehend how Tom is feeling, what he likes and what he is thinking.

- *Social/emotional*: Tom is very clear about what he likes and what he does not like. It is very difficult for Tom to lie or be dishonest because Tom is very literal in his life concepts. When Tom is feeling good about life he is cooperative and wants social contact, when he is confused, afraid or unwell Tom can be difficult to please, aggressive and withdrawn. This means that usually it is easy to tell Tom's emotional status.

- *Cognitive/academic*: Tom appears to operate at the concrete operational level. Knowing this enables Tom's workers to explore learning strategies for Tom that consider his concrete thinking. For example, Tom needs to explore a situation physically to understand how it is made or what it can do. Tom's 'black and white' thinking means that many things are easy to accept. For example: basic rules of hygiene; TV watching times; the rules of a chess game; eating three meals a day.

Tom's difficulties:

○ *Behavioural*: Because it is easy to stay focused on matters of interest for Tom, it is very difficult to encourage Tom to do something that he is not interested in. Also, because Tom doesn't understand 'change', any alteration in Tom's routine or interruption of a ritual can mean fear and confusion for Tom. This could lead to aggressive outbursts or uncooperative behaviour.

○ *Communicative*: Tom loves to talk about his interests but he is not able to understand the interests of others. This means that reciprocal communication is difficult and could lead to Tom having difficulty with relationships.

○ *Social/emotional*: Socially Tom seems unaware of the needs and wants of others. This makes social interaction very difficult. Possibly Tom's lack of eye contact is related to this deficit. Tom can completely miss the cues that another person is giving him.

○ *Cognitive/academic*: 'Black and white' thinking may mean literalness; Tom may have difficulties with 'grey' areas and so on. He needs to take things at a slower pace and have more processing time. It is important that instructions to Tom are given very clearly.

Why does Tom have these difficulties?

According to Wainwright-Sharp and Bryson (1993), visual orienting deficits in high-functioning people with autism may be due to a spatial neglect-like phenomenon. However, Powell and Jordan

(1992) suggest that high-functioning individuals with autism lack a self-concept and, therefore, cannot judge the minds of others. The latter would suggest that some individuals could be taught 'a self-concept' and could also learn better to judge the intentions of others. It is my experience, however, that having a sense of self does not mean that one could automatically develop a sense of other (Lawson 1999b).

Can we help Tom cope with change?

Cesaroni and Garber (1991) note in their study that change for autistic persons appears to be very traumatic, unless the individuals concerned are adequately prepared for it in advance. Unfortunately though, life can be quite unpredictable and advanced warning or preparation for change may not always be possible. Therefore, equipping Tom with a coping strategy for change is a better option long term.

When and how do we execute an intervention for Tom?

Bartak (cited in Rutter and Schopler 1978) found that appropriate intervention skills, learnt during adolescence, continued into adult life. When talking about behaviour modification I believe that ultimate success is assured with the step-by-step reinforcement of a desired outcome. This approach, termed 'shaping', is used when the behaviour is not in the student's behavioural repertoire. Foxx (1982) suggests that target behaviour needs to be heavily reinforced: it should be combined with a discriminative stimulus, physical guidance, imitative prompt and fading (i.e. dissipating slowly by shades and degrees). However, firstly a baseline measurement of the target behaviour needs to be established (Foxx 1982). It is suggested that this occur over a two-week period. Any unusual stimuli should be recorded (e.g. ill health, extra pressure or stress not usual in the individual's daily living).

Wing and Attwood (1987) suggest that the active-but-odd autistic individual (like Tom) is more likely than the aloof autistic individual to want to seek out friendships. This, therefore, is a genuine motivator for wanting to learn social skills and strategies that help create a 'theory of mind'. Also, according to Powell and Jordan (1992), there is some evidence that individuals with AS acquire a theory of mind by 'working it out'.

What about generalising Tom's learnings?

The literature shows that autistic individuals do not generalise their learning, as non-autistic persons do, (Koegel, Rincincover and Egel 1982; Stokes and Baer 1977; Stokes and Osnes cited in Harchik *et al.* 1990). For example, they may learn to sit down at the table to eat at school, but not automatically do the same at home. However, Tom could learn to generalise his learning. For example, he could be taught that it is common practice to sit down to eat, whether he is at home, at school, at a friend's house or in an eating house, such as a café or restaurant.

Prior (1985), Rutter (1983), and Rutter and Schopler (1987) (all cited in Schopler and Mesibov 1992) have found that a basic cognitive deficit exists in children with autism that suggests they only process environmental information through idiosyncratic, stereo-typic strategies (e.g. habitual patterns). For Tom this may mean that he needs to encounter his environment in habitual or routine ways. He may form rules about the way life should be; for example, the traffic should move when the light is green, even if a road accident is causing traffic delay in being able to follow the traffic lights. According to Butera and Haywood (1992), cognitive strategies (e.g. direct teaching concerned with theory via verbal communication) are more likely to produce generalisable learning. This method teaches the higher-functioning autistic individual to 'think' for themselves and gives them a sense of 'control'. For Tom this may mean that he needs to explore the traffic situation and understand why the traffic is not moving. Just 'telling' Tom that the car can't move yet would seem like a direct contradiction to traffic-light rules unless an explanation is demonstrated.

Harchik *et al.* (1992) suggest that maintenance and generalisation tend to occur on cue and independently when the learning has taken place in a structured environment. They also suggest that some behaviours will be maintained 'by naturally existing environmental contingencies'. For Tom this will mean that he needs to practise his learnings often and make direct connections to outcomes and consequences. As outlined earlier, individuals with ASD have difficulties with predicting outcomes as part of either their experiences or their intuition.

Research is demonstrating that all of the differing characteristics fit the differing diagnoses for various individuals along the continuum. No one characteristic is particular to one label. The essential difference (and even this is debatable) is that to gain a diagnosis of AS one needs to have experienced 'normal language development' and have average or above IQ. This begs the questions, 'What is normal language development?' and 'How can a tool developed to assess neuro-typical IQ, be used successfully for those who are not neuro-typical?'

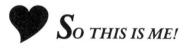 *So THIS IS ME!*

Twiddle dee and twiddle dum,
How on earth have I begun?
I started out all right you see,
But now I question 'who is me?'

Which of these I know so well,
How I wish that I could tell.
If only it could stay the same,
I'd work the rules out for this game.

They call the movie 'Life' you see,
But which is them and which is me?
I know for me the words serve well,
But as for others, who can tell?

I thought I'd got it,
But then came the shock.
You lot knew it,
But I did not!

(Lawson, 1998)

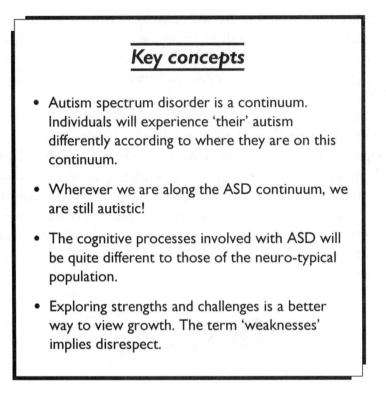

Key concepts

- Autism spectrum disorder is a continuum. Individuals will experience 'their' autism differently according to where they are on this continuum.

- Wherever we are along the ASD continuum, we are still autistic!

- The cognitive processes involved with ASD will be quite different to those of the neuro-typical population.

- Exploring strengths and challenges is a better way to view growth. The term 'weaknesses' implies disrespect.

Point to ponder

I have heard that some folk have difficulty with the giving of a label. 'We are all different', they say. 'Labels separate and can make "difference" a noted factor that might mean "discrimination"'. Well, I must say that if the baked beans in my cupboard were not labelled differently to the tins of cat food, then I would not know how to encounter these foods appropriately! I think labels are useful.

CHAPTER 3

Factors Influencing Autistic Expression

As with all human beings, the behaviour of an individual with autism is influenced not only by being autistic but also by many other factors such as:

- ∘ personality

- ∘ environment

- ∘ health

- ∘ intervention strategies

- ∘ stress and anxiety

- ∘ intellectual ability.

Recognising the influence of these factors will assist in understanding and relating to us as individuals.

How does personality impact upon an individual with ASD? Is it the same as with the neuro-typical population? I tend to think that in lots of ways it is. I have noticed that even though a large number within every population are neuro-typical, individually each appears to be different from the other! What kind of environment enhances positive learning opportunities for an individual with ASD? Is it the same as that for the neuro-typical individual? Ah, I think that for this question the answer has to be 'No'! When you consider how our differing cognitive processes inform our experiences, then it is quite apparent that even within our differing personalities we have distinctive learning styles. What are the common health concerns? It might be tempting to suggest that these are the same for each population, but I tend to think that even here we differ. Therefore, intervention strategies need to account for this. Can 'stress' ever be positive? Well of course it can be. In what ways can stress and anxiety be channelled constructively or effectively reduced? I hope that this book is already answering some of these issues.

Think before assuming!

It is very easy to form an opinion that people within a specific disability grouping will possess the same characteristics. For example: All children with Down Syndrome like music and are affectionate. Although particular disability groups do share some common characteristics, it would be foolish to expect all individuals to behave and act the same way!

Personality

Personality plays a large part in how an individual presents to others. Some people are shy whilst others are extrovert. Some are outgoing, adventurous and curious, others are apprehensive, withdrawn and suspicious. These are personality traits, not aspects of any disorder (unless otherwise diagnosed). When working with us as individuals with ASD, personality must be taken into consideration.

Learning style

We all have individual ways of learning. Think for a moment about your own learning style. Are you a visual learner? Do you think in pictures? Maybe you learn best by interacting with others, and you find textbook, or academic study quite difficult. Some find that they can only study in an environment with the radio playing and themselves surrounded by activity. For others, it has to be complete silence.

Sensory stimulation

Due to the fact that many of us with ASD are easily over-stimulated, a calm classroom environment is useful. A study of academic progress and autism demonstrated that a classroom without posters and pictures on the walls appeared to be a more conducive study environment (Quill, Gurry and Larkin 1989).

What impact do colour, crowds, space, noise, music and time have upon our learning? What about the learning potential of those of us with ASD? How difficult is it to establish just what our intellectual ability is? Consider the following stories.

Assessment for Peter

IQ tests are assessment tools that enable the administrator to score an individual's intelligence quotient (IQ).

Peter is five years old. In order for Peter to attend a particular school for autistic children, he requires an assessment that will demonstrate his IQ is above 55. During the assessment Peter is required to demonstrate that he knows the differences between certain shaped, coloured blocks. The psychologist in this instance has allowed Peter's teacher to sit in on the assessment. Spread before Peter are six coloured blocks of different shapes. 'Peter...give me a circle,' requests the psychologist. Peter sits and appears to be staring out of the window. He does not respond to the request. After asking the question three times the psychologist was about to note Peter's inability to do the task, when the teacher said: 'Peter, give the man the circular block.' Peter picked up the circular block and passed it to the psychologist.

It would have been very easy for the psychologist to state that Peter was not aware of 'his shapes'. If the teacher had not been present to prompt Peter and phrase the statement in 'literal' language terms, Peter would have 'failed' on this part of the assessment and his IQ would have been given as lower than it is.

Assessment for Wendy

When I was assessed in 1994, my overall IQ was said to be 83. The assessor noted that I '...operate at the lower end of average ability...' (see Appendix 5). In the year 2000 I began my PhD programme. This will be my fifth tertiary qualification, four of which I completed within eight years! I doubt that I have an intellectual quadrant graded at 83, when 100 is considered to be average. What this does show, however, is that having autism influences the way I learn and experience life. Therefore, it will impact upon my apparent IQ functioning because IQ tests are written for neuro-typical individuals and are usually administered and scored by neuro-typical means! Let's take a moment to consider these things when we are involved with assessment or with making statements about individuals with autism.

Autistic behaviours

According to Wing (1992) autistic behaviours, as earlier defined by Kanner (1943), consist of: aloofness, indifference towards others, obsessive and compulsive behaviours, resistance to change, repetitive behaviours, lack of expressive language and of 'pretend' play. All psychological theory for understanding ASD is based on what has commonly become known as 'the triad of impairment' (Wing 1992). The triad of impairment suggests that I, as an autistic adult, am impaired socially, in my ability to communicate, and in my ability to imagine.

Impairment implies that I am damaged, ruined, injured or faulty in these three areas! Maybe it's helpful to neuro-typical individuals to conceive of us as so? I only know that this is not helpful to me! I don't believe that I, along with other individuals with ASD, am impaired. We do, however, have a differing learning style to that of the neuro-typically developing population. It is my hope that as you engage with the words in this text, you will come to understand this differing way of learning and, therefore, will be able to explore creatively the 'whys and wherefores' of a variety of behaviours. For example, if a baby cries because it is hungry, do we say it is malformed because it doesn't use speech? 'No' you say, this is natural for a baby because it hasn't yet learned otherwise. I am suggesting that this is also true for many of us who are autistic. We respond in a particular way because we haven't yet learned to do it neuro-typically!

Specific behaviours that parents find 'difficult' appear to be connected to the compulsive, repetitive and obsessive behaviours that are antisocial, embarrassing or a danger to self or others (Asperger Syndrome Parents Group, 1996). So, can we do something about this? I suggest that positive reinforcement of any small move in the direction desired is very rewarding. It is like the child's game of Hot and Cold. However, reinforcement is not the same as rewarding desired behaviour with an offered 'bribe' for change. Rather it is offering 'encouragement' for any sign of behaviour that is desired. The example given relates to one parent's story of reinforcement for her son through complimenting him on his table behaviour. 'You know, Barry, you talk much less at the table than you used to. And, sometimes you listen to what others say and follow the dinner conversation' (cited in Frith 1992, p.197). Apparently this statement brought a marked change in Barry's tendency to monopolise the conversation at dinnertime. Wing points out that such statements or compliments need to be repeated often and follow-up compliments would enhance the learning. We do need, however, to make sure that all instructions are precise and concrete. Keep all instructions simple – set up schedules of importance (e.g. brush hair, brush teeth, etc.).

Health concerns

Sometimes I have real difficulty in 'knowing' if I am tired, unwell, or have reached my physical limit. I can be like a bicycle going at full speed down a hill without the use of any braking system. At the end I crash! It seems to be a fact that many of us require less sleep than the neuro-typical population. However, even when we need to sleep we may not notice, or may not know how to 'switch off' and allow sleep to take its course. Being tired or physically 'run down' may mean that my immune system is weakened and I am prone to becoming unwell. If, however, I don't recognise this, how can I tell others? When the 'usual' behaviour of an individual with autism changes, physical reasons should be explored as a matter of course. Do they have an ear infection? (As a child I suffered greatly with these.) Are they already over-stimulated by too much sensory input? Have they been attending to personal hygiene? Have they any superficial infections, such as boils, splinters, etc?

Never take for granted that an individual with ASD knows or understands what is happening to their body, what, if anything, they need to do about it, and how they need to go about doing that 'something'! Quite often children with ASD cannot tell us that they are unwell. However, they may show changes in behaviour that are indicative of something different happening for them. Learning to know the signs of ill health might be crucial to gaining a quick response. Maybe the child is more cuddly than usual. Maybe they refuse to eat or show little interest in their usually favourite things? Children with ASD may not feel pain in the same way as others. They may not be aware of their status until they are very unwell. When a parent or teacher complains that a child is exhibiting challenging behaviour, physical reasons should be explored first.

Also, from the child's perspective, being singly focused (monotropic) and thinking in closed pictures may mean that a child misses the needed information that informs their experience on being unwell. Therefore, they may need to learn some of the indicators for being unwell. This could mean recognising pain, a raised temperature, vomiting, bleeding, and so on. Once again, these concepts can be role-played at a time when the child is well. They can be explained in social stories, talked about in general conversation, and built into the child's everyday experience of checking in on their 'wellness'.

Intervention

Positive intervention, that which has positively, affirmatively and constructively improved an outcome for me, has been a huge factor in my being able to understand my life experiences. It has also been helpful in my understanding of the behaviour of others. When an intervention is experienced as an interruption, an invasion or an unwelcome advance, however, then it may not be positive, constructive or useful. I think that the way to organise a successful intervention is to gain the individual's cooperation and involvement. When the steps towards the outcome are favourable, in our interest and profitable, we are more likely to want to make the effort. For younger children with ASD, using their obsessions and interests can be a good motivational reward for moving or directing towards the desired outcome. It is important, however, to remember that we may not know our limitations, either by sensory mode or in physical energy.

Stress and anxiety

Anxiety is, perhaps, the biggest factor that dominates my everyday life. I get anxious about how to go to sleep and anxious about being sure I don't miss the time to wake up! It isn't always easy to see my anxiety. I may appear hyped up and excited, so being anxious might not be a consideration. My excitement and enthusiasm can turn rapidly towards anxiety and then fear. This, in turn, can lead to self-stimulatory activity (flapping, flicking, rocking or sucking the roof of my mouth).

I have noticed that some neuro-typical individuals prefer to bite their nails, twist tokens of their hair, bite their lips or smoke cigarettes! I think that the differences between us are not so much in chosen activity, as in what triggers the anxiety. My anxiety is triggered because I find it hard to see the whole picture (I focus on detail); therefore, I miss intent, context and scale. I have problems predicting outcomes. This will mean that I might not see how A plus B can equal C. I find it difficult to cope with change; therefore, some aspects of 'change' can be interpreted as 'terminal' rather than just detour, difference or damage control! For me 'time' doesn't necessarily equate to 'process', and I may need to check in often with already outlined instructions, statements or circumstances. For example, I need to ask the same questions often or I need to check that the answer is 'the same' over and over again.

Relationships

I think for most neuro-typical individuals relationships are based upon mutuality, social priority and wanting others in their life. My need for 'other' is based upon what I need! By this I mean that I relate to other people when it is in my interest to do so. For example, the person may attract me because we share similar interests; I may need the support of another individual to help me with my study skills; I value honesty, commitment and trustworthiness, so, I relate to others with these qualities. I have tended to form over-attachments or no attachment at all. Getting the balance 'right' is rather a difficult task when one's sense of self and of other is confusing, scattered, fragmented and incomplete!

I do have 'friends'. I have just enough friends to share with intimately and feel safe with. These friendships have been constructed over time and are very important to me. However, it has taken work and a lot of 'process' to build these friendships, and they tend to be with others of like mind. I am not interested in relating to folk just for the 'fun' of it. The one aspect about relating that is so essential for my sense of well-being and positive self-esteem is that I am valued, respected and not 'talked down to'! When another human being takes time to walk beside me, interact with me and treat me with dignity I am much more likely to respond to that person in a similar way.

In the past, I suggest, individuals with autism were less likely to form romantic relationships. In fact, it was believed that individuals with autism were not interested in couple relating or that they were not capable of sustaining long-term couple relationships. However, perhaps as the idea of an autism continuum developed and autism was no longer seen as a narrow category of disability, but included more able individuals, the concept of non-relating changed. Today, we have many couples (including myself and my partner) having one or both members with a diagnosis of ASD. I am meeting more and more women who tell me their husband has Asperger Syndrome. I have also met men who tell me their wives have Asperger Syndrome.

It is interesting to me that the couples I see are often complaining about similar issues. They want their partner to be more aware of their needs, give them more affirmation and be more sensitive to family/ couple life concepts. I think it is fair to say that neuro-typical couples are probably facing similar issues. However, possibly due to the differing ways individuals with ASD and neuro-typical individuals are utilising their cognitive processes, the advantage in success rate for relational progress goes to that of the neuro-typical. I don't have statistical evidence to support this claim, only the clinical picture coming from my limited experience. I will say though, that when any individual expects that the person they partner will 'change' and become more loving towards, sensitive to, interested in, or different to, the individual they first encountered and grew to know, they may be in for a disappointment. Limited change to one's personality is possible, but only when one seeks it, wants it and acquires the skills and support to develop it.

For many of us with ASD these ideas may seem inappropriate. We might not think we need to change. We may not find 'change' desirable. We might enjoy our lives the way they are, routines, obsessions, and all. We may also find it very difficult to 'see things' from our partner's perspective. Partners say to me: 'How can I get him/her to change?' 'How can I make him/her understand?' These types of question are not uncommon, but the resources, both personal and professional, may dictate the outcome.

I would suggest that any individual contemplating a long-term relationship should take the time to get to know their prospective partner. Ask yourself the question, 'Am I happy to be waking up next to this person in fifty years' time?' With so many of us, as individuals with ASD, what you see is what you get!

Torment

I couldn't welcome sleep tonight,
The restful peace had ceased.
Just torment tossed became my plight,
As Doona about me creased.

The words of a hymn raged within,
While all without just seemed to shout,
'You're all locked in. There's no way out!'
Oh to have wings and upwards spout!

But there must be a better way, beyond this turmoil sane.
The battered ocean's sandy shore will turn calm again.
Do I have the strength to stand and call the winds to
    blow?
Will tomorrow bring relief, or will it onward go?

I can't remain in this dark storm with edges jagged as,
I want the game of 'tug' to stop and all the pain to pass.
If I allow the rope to drop and exit off the stage,
Will the clouds cease to roll, the storm cease to rage?

I think I know what I must do to calm my troubled breast.
But will I lose a love so dear and can I ride the crest?
Please help me to let this rope go and join in tenderness,

The only safe way out of here is if we both say 'yes'.

I need to leave this forbidden land and journey on my way.
I'm asking you to hold my hand and with me stand to
     pray.
For strength to do what is right and courage to battle on.
To end my plight I must take flight, 'adjure my friend'
     lulay.

(Lawson 2000)

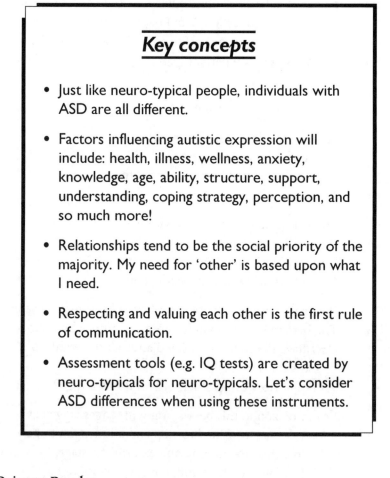

Key concepts

- Just like neuro-typical people, individuals with ASD are all different.

- Factors influencing autistic expression will include: health, illness, wellness, anxiety, knowledge, age, ability, structure, support, understanding, coping strategy, perception, and so much more!

- Relationships tend to be the social priority of the majority. My need for 'other' is based upon what I need.

- Respecting and valuing each other is the first rule of communication.

- Assessment tools (e.g. IQ tests) are created by neuro-typicals for neuro-typicals. Let's consider ASD differences when using these instruments.

Point to Ponder

Sometimes it seems that the only way to succeed in a relationship is not to relate at all!

CHAPTER 4

Obsessive, Compulsive and Self-injurious Behaviour

Obsessive behaviour

Obsessive or compulsive behaviours (persistent or irrational thoughts, wishes and actions that may be uncontrollable or repetitive) may be motivated either by pleasure or by anxiety. Sometimes, simply because the individual with ASD does not know how to finish a repetitive activity they initiated, it can lead into anxiety even though it began as pleasure. The important thing to consider is that for whatever reason if anxiety is suspected then the individual might need help, to refocus and calm down.

How do we decide that an action or behaviour is 'obsessive'? According to my dictionary of psychology (Reber 1995) an obsession is 'any idea that haunts, hovers and constantly invades one's consciousness. Obsessions are seemingly beyond one's "will" and awareness of their inappropriateness is of little or no avail.' However, I would suggest that obsessive behaviour or obsessions might be born from two different sources.

Anxiety-driven obsessions

This might be labelled obsessive-compulsive disorder (OCD) and tends to be characterised by recurrent and persistent thoughts, ideas, and feelings. These are accompanied by repetitive, ritualised behaviours. Attempts to resist this type of obsession might lead to increased anxiety and tension. Apparently, recent evidence suggests that OCD is associated with damage to or dysfunctions of the basal ganglia, cingulate gyrus and the prefrontal cortex (Reber 1995). OCD may respond well to anti-obsessional medication.

Monotropic interests

These might mean that rather than being able to occupy oneself with a variety of interests, which cancels out any need to be obsessive with one interest, we can only be occupied with one constant interest at any one time. This could, therefore, be interpreted as being 'obsessive'. If an individual is monotropic by design, then they are not designed to be polytropic. This means it would be very difficult indeed to have more than one (mono) interest at any one time.

Such 'obsessions' can be useful when reframed, contained and placed into a (poly) context of everyday life. As individuals with ASD we may need help to do this. I can think of one lad who loved to open and close all the curtains in his mother's home, and he could do so for hours. His obsession was not born from anxiety or boredom. He simply enjoyed the experience and loved to repeat it over and over again. However, for his mum's sanity and to free some time for her son, we put some boundaries around this activity. We said that he was allowed to open and close the curtains in his room only, for ten minutes after school. He then had other singular activities that Mum scheduled for him. His obsession could be used as a reward for doing other things and, in this way, family life was less stressful.

Compulsions

In many ways I think it is understandable that as an individual with ASD I have a variety of compulsions. These are acts or behaviours that I feel compelled to do. Maybe within the neuro-typical population there are also a variety of compulsions? I have noted that people can feel 'compelled' to say 'please', 'thank you', 'hello' and 'goodbye'. They may feel compelled to correct someone's speech, dress, manners or behaviour, if it differs from their own. Within the world of ASD, however, we tend to have different needs that compel us.

I have a need for order, therefore, I constantly feel compelled to arrange and order my clothes, furniture, tableware, and so on. If 'things' are not in their right place I may find it difficult to know what to do next, move into the next part of a conversation, work out the next part or aspect of a procedure, and so on. I believe my being monotropic has much to do with my compelling needs. I am singly channelled and need to move and act in an orchestrated, single-minded fashion. This is very enabling for me and is probably the basis for my rules, rituals, and repetitive behaviours.

Self-injury

According to Mohr and Sharpley (1985) self-injurious behaviour (SIB) needs to be treated with immediate and effective intervention. Apparently, SIB can be categorised into three types: medical, psychodynamic and behavioural (Mohr and Sharpley 1985). Medical intervention is commonly used for SIB, with developmentally delayed individuals. However, studies show that this method is rarely successful (Picker, Poling and Parker 1979; Ross and McKay, both cited in Mohr and Sharpley 1985). One report concluded that 'medical treatment may be neither necessary nor sufficient' (Fawell, cited in Mohr and Sharpley 1985, p.143). However, in a direct comparison of psychoanalysis with behavioural intervention, results showed that 'providing comfort and reassurance, treatment was successful' (Lovaas et al. cited in Mohr and Sharpley 1985, p.143). It is my experience that psychoanalysis for individuals with ASD isn't helpful. The research shows that cognitive interventions, however, do work well (Attwood 2000). Some medication can also be helpful in some situations for some individuals. It is important to note, however, that minimal dosage appears to work, rather than recommended dosage that neuro-typical individuals may benefit from (Grandin 1996).

Mohr and Sharpley (1985) suggest that mild punishment, over-correction and reinforcement can be successful in the reduction and elimination of SIB. I have a problem with the concept of 'mild punishment', however, because I wonder how we can decide what 'mild' means? It might mean different things to different people. If an action is being performed as a means of communication, then 'punishment' hasn't any place here at all. The use of verbal reprimands such as 'NO' and short phrases to tell the autistic person what to do, however, could be useful. For example, 'hand still, hand down' at the same time as placing hand down on to table, knee or lap, were first resources; encouragement and reinforcement took the form of 'good boy, lovely still hand', etc. frequently expressed, (e.g. once per ten seconds of appropriate behaviour delivered intermittently).

It is very important that an ASD individual does not become over-stimulated or experience sensory overload. Sensory overload can be a reason for anxiety and consequent inappropriate, self-abusive or aggressive behaviour. I was not really into self-injury as a response to overload, but I certainly moved into aggression that was visited upon others, as a direct outcome of sensory overload. As I grew older, I became more aware of what my limits were. However, conveying this information to others hasn't always been easy!

Sometimes head banging and knuckle nibbling, tantrums, or outbursts happen as a way of letting someone know enough is enough! It is wise to spot the signs before it gets to this stage so that alternatives can be explored. This might mean time or space alone. Sometimes soft familiar music is helpful; relaxation and breathing exercises work for some people. I find that I need lots of space from demand, and frequenting the 'outside' world often, is very useful. I can also experience a lot of sensory input (noise, lights, talking, questions, movement, crowds, activity, busyness, and even my own thinking processes concerning decision making) as overwhelming. I quickly become agitated when these things are too much for me. If an individual with ASD is also intellectually 'dis-abled', then self-injury is one way to 'relieve' the pain from sensory overload. When overload is removed and the individual is restored to a place of equilibrium, self-injury might cease. Self-injury can actually become a habit and can almost seem to act as an 'enjoyable' friend if it isn't curtailed! At least it is something I can choose and can appear to have control over.

The following are some key signs to look for if you suspect overload:

- pacing up and down

- covering ears with one's hands

- screaming

- excessive spinning or rocking of one's body

- loud verbalisation

- total withdrawal

- aggression

- head banging

- self-injury

- irritation.

The following strategies for preventing or overcoming sensory overload might be useful. First, it is important to structure a child or young person's day so that sensory input is minimised and controlled. Second, the ASD individual might need a regular set 'time out' occasions where they can sit or be safely, without being swamped with people, noise or demands (e.g. 20 minutes on the mat with the other children in the classroom and then 5 minutes on their beanbag behind a dividing screen away from other children). Sometimes an ASD individual can work or play well for a short period of time, but then they need a break. This period may vary for different individuals. The break-time, however, will always mean a time apart from sensory stimuli. Third, if an individual still moves on into overload, then they require a quiet non-interactive environment where they can 'calm down' and gain a sense of sensory restoration. If an individual finds it difficult to inform an appropriate other of 'how they are feeling', then a number of steps can be taken. These are outlined in Chapter 8, where you will find many useful practical suggestions.

I'm safe... Am I?

Your words echo within my head.
What was it you exactly said?
Something about 'turning over a new leaf'
Taking a shower, my bed and beneath?

I ran out into the garden.
You said loudly 'Come back now'.
I had the leaf, and then,
You said you'd make me, somehow.

I offered you my leaf. It was all shiny and new.
You knocked it out of my hand,
It fell swiftly and hit the harsh ground.
What was it that I was meant to do?

Whatever it was,
I was sure I'd do wrong.
My room, my sanctuary.
I'd best move along.

I pushed myself past you,
Just keen to escape.
Your hands reached to grab me,
'Oh no you don't, mate'.

My hands went to my ears,
As your voice was raised.
I walked in small circles
While your eyes just gazed.

'So, getting off with it again are we?'
Your voice splurted sound.
Life is too difficult,
I'll just walk around!

(Lawson 1999)

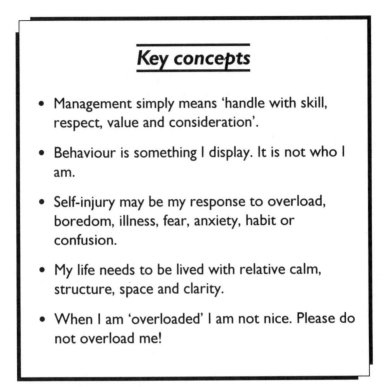

Key concepts

- Management simply means 'handle with skill, respect, value and consideration'.

- Behaviour is something I display. It is not who I am.

- Self-injury may be my response to overload, boredom, illness, fear, anxiety, habit or confusion.

- My life needs to be lived with relative calm, structure, space and clarity.

- When I am 'overloaded' I am not nice. Please do not overload me!

Point to ponder

One way to engage with autistic children and, therefore, encourage early learning is by way of early intervention programmes. Children with autism respond very well to 'concrete learning' situations and behavioural management strategies (Attwood 1992).

PART II

The Spectrum of Autism
and Issues Related to Stress

CHAPTER 5

ASD Cognition and Family Stress
What Might This Mean in Practice?

Neuro-typicality versus ASD

As previously suggested, even though individuals with ASD may not be intellectually disabled, we process stimuli differently to neuro-typical individuals. In fact, many non-autistic individuals with an intellectual disability are very neuro-typical in their understanding of the world. In everyday situations where communication is part of the interaction with another, a person with ASD may not interpret the situation as easily as a neuro-typical person might. In fact we may not appreciate the situation at all. However, due to our usual concrete thinking ability we benefit from 'straight talk', concrete analogies, guidance without criticism, and some help in decision making (Attwood 1998).

Individual neuro-typical cognition appears to rely upon the normal and natural ability to understand and interact with the world around oneself. ASD individuals do not process information in the same way as neuro-typical individuals. This book postulates that, in fact, neuro-typical processing and knowledge application could in itself be a cause for conflict. For example, neuro-typical understanding of metaphor and simile is learned quite easily and generalised to other settings, whereas for us, as individuals with ASD, this is not so.

To explore this more, consider the following example. When a child with ASD is engaged in behaviour that a parent wants to curtail, the parent might say 'You can't do that!' Unfortunately the child *is doing it* and, due to the child's literal translation, will most likely not understand the instruction as intended by the parent. The child may even consider the parent to be stupid! But when a parent says 'Stop, come away from…and move over to me please', then the child with ASD understands what is expected of them and is more likely to comply. If a parent does not understand the literality of their child with ASD, then they will interpret their child's lack of compliance as wilful disobedience. Stress and anxiety for all will only increase.

Another example of this is the following: By shouting 'We don't have yelling in the house' and the boys are yelling, the youth with ASD, who takes words literally, might assume you are lying or are stupid, because probably all three of you are yelling in the house! Understanding literality as an active component of ASD will enable parents to respond more confidently towards their child with ASD, who in return will feel safer and less likely to demonstrate self-injurious or destructive behaviour.

For some parents (whose children have some symptoms of autism but do not completely fit the criteria for a diagnosis) life must seem to be very cruel indeed. Such children may be given the label PDD-NOS (pervasive developmental delay not otherwise specified). As Amanda Golding said to me when I met her at a conference in 1999, this adds to parental stress because their child is neither 'disabled' nor 'normal'. There is much confusion around this term. It indicates that a child has difficulties of an 'autistic' nature but does not qualify for many of the services on offer to children with 'autism'. Rimland (1993) suggests that even the term PDD is 'concocted by psychiatrists to cover up the fact that they don't know what your child does have' (p.73). This belief is quite distressing and offers no reassurance to parents at all. In fact it can only add to the weight of grief, confusion and stress that parents will experience.

There is some research that suggests that even within the recognised 'autism spectrum' some parents will experience greater stress and less ability to cope, due to the fact that their child does not have an intellectual disability (Sharpley *et al.* 1997). This may be due to the fact that individuals with an intellectual disability qualify for many support services. This means that for the 30 per cent of children with ASD who are not intellectually disabled, resources may be limited or simply not available. Perhaps this is one reason why stress levels appear to be higher for the parents of ASD children who are not intellectually disabled.

Appropriate supports for parents

Sharpley *et al.* (1997) suggest that stress for parents of a child with autism could be lowered if appropriate supports were in place. For example:

- self-help support groups for parents and/or family members
- discussion groups for AS adolescents and high-functioning children with autism
- increased education and in-service training for professionals
- increased amenities, counselling and respite for families.

They also suggest that coping skills would be enhanced through such mediums as outlined above. This would happen as a consequence of parents increasing in confidence and self-esteem due to their feeling less isolated, better informed, more fully supported and more adequately provided for.

Parental anxiety, respite and foster parenting/grandparenting

According to Briggs and Fitzpatrick (1994) one of the reasons that some individuals suffer neglect and emotional or physical abuse is because the parents themselves are overwhelmed with their own problems. In both New Zealand and England there has been an occasion where a parent has murdered their ASD teenage child, because they felt they had no other option. Maybe if appropriate ASD trained respite-care services, greater understanding and ASD support had been available these young people might be alive today. When individuals with ASD can be appropriately catered for, and parents given some 'time off', then family tensions tend to lessen. Some family support services even offer a holiday break for families. This is often subsidised by state or community funding, which means less expense and less worry for the family.

When a parent is suffering from severe anxiety and this is affecting their parenting ability, there may be sufficient concern to take the individual with ASD into short-term foster care. Although most children can feel a sense of grief and abandonment when taken away from home and all that is familiar (Briggs and Fitzpatrick 1994), individuals with ASD may not appear to demonstrate these emotions. However, when an overall picture is put together it is often noted that the individual with ASD can display inappropriate behaviours, aggression or self-injury as their way of expressing their discomfort. It is important, therefore, that moving away from home and into a residential setting be seen as a last resort. For older teenagers and young adults who would normally be expected to leave home the procedure may need to happen over time, possibly starting later and with lots of support for the individual and the family.

Appropriate supports for individuals with ASD

As an intellectually able individual with an autism spectrum disorder I was inclined to think that my difficulties in everyday life were because I was not as intelligent as other people. The only way that I could cope with my daily confusion and frustration was by living according to rules, rituals and routines.

I often avoid social gatherings. I prefer my own company and I totally miss the cues for ordinary social interaction (e.g. polite conversation in public places). Panic attacks, social phobia and other fears and phobias may dominate my existence.

> I find it difficult to know how to maintain a conversation… unless it's about a favoured topic of mine. I also get over loaded with all the sensory information that comes from people in a social situation, such as conversational noise, movement of people, clothing, doors and so on. The only time I enjoy social occasions are when they occur on my terms with friends that I know and trust. I can plan these times, enter and exit when I want to and I can be myself. (Lawson 1998b, p.3)

For many people, talking and sharing in conversation is an everyday fact of life that requires little thought. If, however, they are going for an interview, or to an appointment that requires careful conversational consideration (the 3 C's), then they usually take more time to think and construct what they want to say. If we are talking to neuro-typical individuals (folk who don't have an intellectual, social or communication disability) then conversational chit-chat (the other 3 C's) might be appropriate. However, when you are talking with individuals with an autism spectrum disorder, the three C's you choose can make a difference as to whether or not you or we are understood. Understanding is the first 'key' to good communication.

If you are a person with ASD then quite likely you will take people's words literally. For example, teacher says: 'Pull your socks up, John, or you won't make it into the team.' John bends down and pulls his socks up. The teacher is then irritated by John and calls him a 'smarty pants'. John replies that he doesn't have any smarties in his pants. Teacher sends John to the headteacher because of John's insolence. John doesn't know what all the fuss is about; he is missing his favourite period at school, the time on the computer, and he becomes very upset. John comes home with a note from his teacher that requires him to do detention for insolent behaviour!

Taking words literally and thinking in closed pictures is what I, and many other individuals with ASD, do naturally. As an intellectually able mature adult I understand most metaphorical expressions. However, as a child with ASD, metaphor made no sense to me. Literality is part of the autistic condition.

Appropriate interventions and increased awareness of how having a different learning style impacts upon the individual concerned and their associated others is crucial. Stress is associated with misunderstanding, mismanagement and being misinformed! Stress for individuals with ASD can be lowered by a number of responses outlined here. However, each individual's learning style should be noted, personality and sensory issues must also be a consideration.

For parents and family members stress can be alleviated by having others understand them and their situation. Respite, appropriate support and financial backing may also be factors. Difference is always uncomfortable. We all like to be amongst that which is familiar, predictable and comfy. Imagine how uncomfortable it would be if you took words and people literally? You would so often feel let down, disappointed, lied to, and so on. How could you ever depend on someone? Change is uncomfortable for all of us but, for individuals with ASD, who interpret their world literally, change can be terrifying.

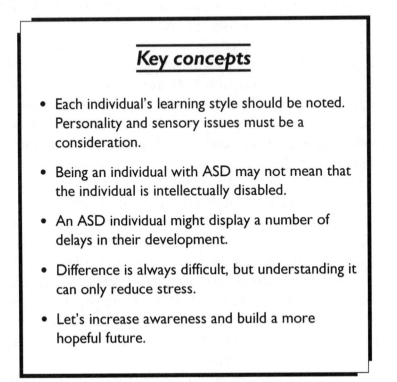

Key concepts

- Each individual's learning style should be noted. Personality and sensory issues must be a consideration.

- Being an individual with ASD may not mean that the individual is intellectually disabled.

- An ASD individual might display a number of delays in their development.

- Difference is always difficult, but understanding it can only reduce stress.

- Let's increase awareness and build a more hopeful future.

Point to ponder

Many families living with individuals with ASD will already have spent many years living and coping with the situation. As research has shown, stress increases with time (Dyson, 1993). Therefore, adolescence will be especially difficult because of stress associated with the 'time' factor, anticipated transition (e.g. puberty; the last years of school, beginning employment or considering the future) and developmental stages for other family members as they age.

CHAPTER 6

Anxiety

Overview

Families with an autistic child frequently experience anxiety and depression as a response to insufficient support and understanding of their child's disability. *Anxiety* is seen and felt as a result of inner conflict. It is the term given to describe the response of the human organism to perceived threat to one's welfare or safety (Clinebell 1991). *Depression*, for the purpose of this text, will be thought of as a term describing a state of sadness, helplessness and despair (Kennedy and Charles 1994).

I suggest that the triggers for anxiety in the neuro-typical population might be different to those within the ASD population. I also suggest that anxiety might be experienced differently for each population. This chapter will briefly explore some of the components of anxiety for both neuro-typical individuals and individuals with ASD.

Family Life and Autism

As already stated, in the past autism was thought to be the result of poor parenting, particularly by mothers. Today's thinking about ASD suggests that it is probably a variant or an atypicality of the central nervous system (CNS), genetically based (Prior 1992) and nothing at all to do with poor parenting. The CNS refers to the brain and spinal cord, and being 'genetically based' means that ASD, in most cases, will be genetically predisposed. Research is showing that a number of genes need to be acting together for the full syndrome of ASD to occur (Marks 1999).

Obtaining a diagnosis of ASD

Often the local doctor is the family's first port of call. However, for many families locating a diagnosis before the age of three is very difficult. Some families have not been able to obtain a diagnosis until their child was much older. Such families may feel isolated, confused, unsupported and very anxious. Appropriate intervention by a professional can assist in lowering stress levels and increases the opportunity for enhancing a psychological sense of well-being. Early intervention, counselling, parent and sibling support groups, education, raising community awareness and lobbying for change to government policy, are some of the ways that professionals can positively aid these families.

'Parental grieving of childhood disability is an experience which is complex, long-lasting and fluctuating in nature' (Foy 1997, p.39). How distressing it must be for any parent to know the joy of pregnancy, of giving birth, and then to watch their hopes and dreams diminish as their family life is subject to confusion and subsequent erosion. For many parents it's a long haul to eventual diagnosis. Sometimes a parent has been to many different doctors, social workers, and other professionals, but to no avail. Often they are left with feelings of isolation, despondency and the belief that they must be terrible parents.

Triggers for ASD?

The research suggests that ASD is predisposed genetically, but what might the triggers be? I think there could be many and I think they might be different for differing individuals. However, I will briefly discuss the most topical at the time of writing this book.

Vaccines (measles, mumps and rubella, MMR)

It goes without saying that most parents want to give their children the best chance in life. Taking care of themselves during pregnancy, eating a balanced diet, not smoking or taking alcohol, and aiming to 'give birth' appropriately, and so on, kick starts the process. Then we are told that our children do best when they are breast-fed. This gives them access to the necessary antibodies that will help protect their health during their first few months of life. Next we are told that our children need to be vaccinated to protect them against terrible and deadly diseases. In the past single vaccinations have proved efficient and many once-feared and deadly diseases became almost extinct in Western society. However, then came the triple vaccination process whereby at least three vaccines were administered at the same time (MMR). In the year 2000, our Western society is in turmoil over the use of the MMR. With the current vaccination crisis how can we be sure that our children will not be harmed by such a vaccination?

ASD and various triggers that might be implicated are currently being debated. Many families no longer trust the MMR triple vaccination process because of its implication as a trigger for autism. According to Professor Vijendra Singh, reporting to the 2000 International Public Conference on Vaccination in Virginia, this vaccination can damage protein in the brain. He suggests that research indicates the myelin sheath surrounding the nerves in the brain may not develop properly as a result of this vaccination. This leads to the type of brain abnormality displayed in autism. His report states that 'the MMR might trigger an autoimmune reaction in some children. This, in turn, could cause antibodies in the blood to attack the brain' (*Herald Sun*, 15 September 2000).

CLINICAL FEATURES

According to Shattock and Savery (1997) some children given the MMR vaccination who have been shown to react negatively to it present the following clinical picture:

> The suggestion has been made that, in some cases of autism, the measles element of the MMR programme could be a significant factor. Evidence has already been published which links measles particles with the greatly increased incidence of Crohn's Disease, which has been seen over recent years. Work is currently in progress to identify the presence of these same particles in the lower intestinal walls of some people with autism. If present, these particles would, certainly, increase the permeability of the intestinal walls so that increased levels of gut derived peptides would reach the blood stream and, ultimately, the blood brain barrier. In those children where such a sequence of events is

believed to have taken place, parents report a rapid and serious reaction, within hours or at least within 2 days, to the vaccine. Epileptic fits; coma; incessant screaming; rapid loss of bowel function and control are all reported and this is with concomitant appearance or increase of autistic behaviours.

In another, smaller, group of subjects, the clinical picture is different. There is no sudden, rapid or spectacular event but the child still loses abilities very soon after the MMR injection. Although it may not have been mentioned initially, subsequent questioning frequently reveals that there has been a quite serious illness some weeks afterwards. Our suggestion is that the disruption caused to the meninges which form an integral part of the blood brain barrier is such that high levels of peptides which may be circulating in the blood can now reach the CNS.

It is worth mentioning that such children seem to do very much better than the majority of children with autism in the comparatively short term. It is interesting to speculate that those children who are reported as making spectacular recoveries might be from this group. It may well be that, with time, the attenuated strain of mumps is eventually eliminated by the immune system so that the meninges recover and the blood brain barrier can operate as effectively as before. Whatever the form of therapy being employed with such children will be credited with responsibility for this cure.

I would suggest, therefore, that if there is any history of autism in the family that parents talk to their GPs about the risks of vaccination. One needs to be fully informed before making a decision on this issue. Some GPs and others believe that single-dose vaccinations are preferable to multi-dose vaccinations. I think it is also wise to wait until a child is well, strong and old enough to cope with vaccination. This might mean waiting until a child is at least two years old. Parents should always consult their doctors if they have any concerns.

Diet

Many parents are exploring the idea that diet plays a role in their child's autism. Shattock (1990) suggests that some children with autism are suffering from 'leaky gut' syndrome. He states that when young children, in particular, have foods with dairy products, gluten and casein removed from their diet, then their autistic behaviours decrease. I have spoken to many parents who agree with him!

However, it is important to give any child as much of a balanced diet as is possible. If a child is only eating wheat cereal with milk, then eliminating this from the diet needs careful consideration. Changing the diet for individuals with ASD needs to be a subtle process. Introducing the chosen non-dairy, gluten and casein-free foods, over time and in an acceptable way, is very important. Sometimes having a dietician or paediatrician overseeing this process can be helpful. For parents and children this whole process may need support. Teachers and carers need to be fully informed.

Implications?

It is known that some women have the gene for breast cancer. However, not all of these women will develop breast cancer. This suggests that there is a trigger for the disease. Therefore, women are encouraged to eat healthily, not smoke, deal with anxiety and stress in their lives and take particular care of themselves. I believe that this is also true for the spectrum of autism. Vaccination and diet have been suggested as such triggers; maybe there are others. The forum on this topic is not conclusive. The implications for family life, however, are many.

Understanding the issues for siblings

Being a sibling of someone with ASD can mean different things for different people. However, I suggest that many individuals will experience the following:

- ○ loss of hope for a regular family (why didn't I get a 'normal' brother/sister?)

- ○ loss of regular sibling interaction (my brother/sister can't relate 'normally' to me)

- ○ the fight for an individual identity (my brother/sister monopolises my parents' time – where do I fit in?)

- issues of shared and appropriate responsibility (my brother/sister never takes responsibility, I get blamed for everything)
- teamwork versus separateness (I always have to look out for my brother/sister, I never get time for me)
- issues around dealing with reality (facing the challenges of being a 'different' family, facing the challenges of having disability within the family).

Support for siblings of children with ASD is a crucial aspect to aid healthy typical development. Neuro-typical individuals will process life experiences differently to those of us within the ASD population. Therefore siblings will need to understand that their ASD brothers and sisters are different. If individuals only use neuro-typical visual perception, cognitive perception, group perception, spatial perception and affective perception, then this might mean that non-autistic siblings will find ASD very hard to understand, accommodate and come to terms with. Siblings may also benefit from specific sibling support such as listening and taking time to know them. It is imperative for other family members to understand the different ASD cognitive processes (explored in Chapter 1). Again these are:

- literality
- monotropism, or being singly channelled (serial concepts)
- thinking in closed pictures
- non-social priorities
- non-generalised learning
- issues with time and motion
- issues with predicting outcomes
- difficulties with theory of mind (empathy lacks and empathy gaps).

Any facilitator of a sibling support group, whether working with children or older individuals, needs firstly to understand the processes informing their own world or population and then those informing that of the individual with ASD. This information can assist in bridge building between the two cultures.

When siblings affectively understand their ASD sibling, then they are part of the way to understanding their own needs. The world of typicality is the one non-autistic individuals usually belong to. They may need support in discovering this world and learning to feel part of it. Finding other individuals that share their hopes and fears is a good beginning to 'normalising' their life. Having access to regular support, specific sibling time with parents and family without their ASD brother or sister, learning openly to express their needs, wants, hopes, anger, frustration and dreams in a healthy manner, are part of the process to lessen guilt and anxiety and to foster healthy development.

How might individuals with ASD experience anxiety?

First, it is important to distinguish between ASD and intellectual disability. For some professionals autism and intellectual disability are seen to be synonymous terms that are interchangeable. This is not the case. As already stated, intellectual disability occurs in 70 per cent of individuals with autism. However, this leaves 30 per cent of them with average or above average intelligence who, although displaying severe communication and social deficits, are not taken seriously by many in our community. This alone can be a trigger for deep anxiety.

It is always important to know an individual well enough to be able to detect differences or deviations from that individual's particular or usual behaviour. Anxiety in individuals with ASD may present differently for each person. Knowing how the individual behaves 'normally' or usually is necessary in order to understand when any particular behaviour is unusual for that individual. As a matter of course any other reason for unusual behaviour must be explored. For example, could the individual be physically unwell? Have there been any changes to the individual's expected environment, programme, personal encounters, and so on. If such instances are eliminated and the behaviour still exhibits, then anxiety from other causes may be considered. Anxiety for individuals with ASD may be experienced and exhibited in a number of ways. This might be inwardly, leading to tension, headaches, tummy upsets, skin rashes and obsessive inclination toward repetitive behaviours. It may also be experienced and exhibited outwardly, leading to self-injurious behaviour or to aggressive outbursts.

What might trigger anxiety for individuals with ASD?

For me, being monotropic in a multi-channelled world, can lead to huge anxiety. I am so often expected to process more than one thing at any one time. I find this demanding and because it is so difficult to do, I can become anxious even thinking of the event. This can mean that I might respond in a number of ways. For example, I might close off and turn away. I might only understand part of an instruction and fail to get it right, or I might react anxiously, developing headaches, joint pain or skin rashes.

I can become just as anxious about what I do not know, as about what I do know. I am always asking questions, checking in with my family to make sure the information I was given is still correct. This can happen as frequently as every few minutes. The following two stories may help explore the issue of anxiety and ASD a bit more.

In the playground

> Joel, a nine-year old boy with an autism spectrum delay, goes to a regular school. At recess Joel is expected to go outside with the other children from his class and 'play'. However, Joel does not have social priorities, is very literal in his understanding, and is also monotropic. Therefore, for Joel, 'play' with other children, with all of their unspoken rules, rituals and social expectations, is a very traumatic experience and one that he would rather avoid. For Joel, every time he approaches the ending of morning, lunchtime or afternoon school, and he knows that the bell will ring soon for recess, he experiences a set of emotional and physical happenings that are very unpleasant. His heart begins to beat faster, his hands become sweaty, he hums incessantly to crowd out his thoughts about recess and he attempts to crawl under his desk where he hopes the teacher will not see him.
>
> Joel's anxiety cannot be relieved by reassurance because reassurance will not enable him to work out or acquire the social understanding that will allow him to 'play'. Dragging Joel out

from under the table and insisting that he go outside with all the other children will only increase his anxiety levels, and he may react with physical violence. His 'challenging' behaviour might then be seen as defiance, and he may be further penalised or 'punished'; this will only further increase his anxiety. Anxiety, one of our natural defence resources, if it goes unrecognised may become either internalised (leading to ill health, skin irruptions, headaches, phobias, obsessions, repetitive behaviours, and so on) or externalised (leading to self-injury, physical aggression, withdrawal, problems with eating, sleeping, toileting, and so on). Joel's only way through his anxiety about recess and outside play in the playground is for him to gain the social under-standing that will then enable him to join in with his peers and give him confidence (see Chapter 10).

In the exam room

When I was a university student, I was given a number of written examinations. During my first year I found this extremely stressful and suffered with immense anxiety. I first encountered this kind of response to exams when I was eleven and experienced what was then called the 'eleven plus' exam. This exam was given to establish ability and potential. For children who did well, there was an offer of grammar school (a more academic institution of learning); for children who were not so successful, secondary modern school was the way to go.

I was given this test under exam conditions, even though, at the time, I was an in-patient at a large city hospital. I was not prepared for this test, nor was it explained appropriately to me. I sat in front of my upsidedown paper, and eventually the teacher said: 'OK Wendy, you can now turn the page.' So, I did! My being literal meant that this was where my understanding ended. I sat with the page turned but proceeded no further than that. I sat in front of that exam paper throughout the entire exam period and did not write any other information, apart from my name (because I was told to write my name). I rocked back and forth on my chair, I stared at the clock on the wall and became increasingly anxious at the thought of what I could be doing back in the ward. I was used to the hospital routine, having been there for several months, and my mind was full of what were my usual activities! As the minutes ticked past on the clock in the room, so my anxiety increased. My heart rate increased, I began to develop a skin irritation, I wet myself, I snapped three pencils and the teacher had to ask me, several times, to stop rocking on the legs of my chair. Needless to say, at the end of that afternoon, I hadn't completed the exam and I didn't pass my eleven-plus!

As an older teenager and now as an adult I have developed many coping strategies so that my anxiety can be managed. However, I still get caught out by my literal translation of words. For example, at a recent conference where I was one of the keynote speakers, I noticed that all of the front seats in the auditorium had 'reserved' labels on them. So I made sure that I sat in the seat behind and left the front row seats vacant. Just after the first session had commenced a gentleman from the front row came up to me and advised me that, in fact, the reserved seats were for the speakers, including me. It caused me extreme anxiety to have to move seats when a speaker had begun to speak. I am of the mind that it is rude to do this once proceedings have begun and I felt very uncomfortable. This discomfort and slight annoyance with the organisers for not labelling the seats with names stayed with me and impacted negatively upon my own presentation later that day.

How can the professional help?

1.   As professionals we can help parents to understand ASD and the concrete strategies that their children need. For example, step-by-step instructions that let an individual know exactly what is required of them. We can aim to make sure that all information is complete, accurate and up to date. This will help children and adults to respond to their environment in a more positive way and individual stress levels to be kept to a minimum.

2.   Respite, short-term and long-term, should be available to give family members a break. However, all respite services for ASD should be staffed by ASD-trained individuals.

3. When working as part of an interdisciplinary team, professionals who are 'autism aware' will be able to offer an educated response across a wide range of issues to families.

4. Support groups for parents and siblings are a major factor in promoting and maintaining 'family wellness'.

5. Lobbying local government on behalf of families with a child placed on the autism continuum will help to ensure ongoing policy commitment.

Mental health outcomes – Overview

Mental health problems are often referred to as 'mental illness'. According to Payne (1996), 'mental illness' conjures up certain images for people. In Western society whenever the word 'mental' is used in connection with illness, it is often thought of as synonymous with the word 'mad'. For example, expressions such as 'they're a mental case' or 'he's gone mental' and 'she's throwing a mental' are common in everyday conversations. This being so, in order to be correctly understood and to displace fears caused by such beliefs, when an individual presents with the characteristics of anxiety in their personality, it is important to address their fears, explore the presenting issues and map out the appropriate interventions and services. Research is showing that anxiety can be a precursor to further issues, such as depression and mental illness (Ghaziuddin 2000).

Anxiety issues

Issues for the neuro-typical family member

According to Kellerman and Burry (1991) it is essential that we understand just how the management of anxiety in personality functioning affects:

-   operation of cognitive controls (ability to problem solve)

-   achievement of potential levels of intellectual functioning

-   symptom formation (physical and emotional characteristics of anxiety)

- subjective distress (distress that appears unfounded).

If the anxiety is not regulated or managed adaptively, then problems may emerge that include:

- depression, withdrawal or inhibition of effort

- school failure, job loss, neglectful parenting or relationship trauma

- irritability and aggression

- passivity or dependency.

Issues for the parent/professional

It is important to understand how the anxiety is experienced. Is the anxiety consciously experienced, acted out, or somatised?

- If consciously experienced, what is the subjective level of distress?

- Does the anxiety generate fantasy, reinforce passivity, or stimulate activity?

- Are phobias or panic states developed?

- Are obsessions developed to generalised anxiety feelings?

Assessment

Usually an individual is referred to a professional psychologist because the anxiety is interfering with the person's everyday life and they can no longer ignore it. They may have developed a history of substance abuse, outbursts of violence or complete social withdrawal. Relationship and employment issues are common and the client may feel trapped in a world of utter turmoil.

During allotted appointment times assessment can be conducted to uncover the issues for the client. As they are engaged in conversation there will be opportunity for client disclosure, goal setting and appropriate intervention (O'Connor, Wilson and Thomas 1991). Even during the first interview the emotional state of the client can be observed. This can be assessed through noticing the client's speed of speech (i.e. too fast or too slow, without motivation), emotional state, (are they crying or super cool?) and thought content (e.g. are they rational or contradictive?) (Kennedy and Charles 1994).

After a short while observation of the client's defence systems, coupled with other observations, can inform a tentative hypothesis. Once this is established possible interventions for the client can be explored. Tentative outcomes can be suggested, long-term recommendations made and follow-up interventions adjusted.

Specific issues

Individuals who are experiencing 'anxiety neurosis' (a subclass of anxiety disorders characterised by recurrent periods of intense anxiety, e.g. panic disorders, generalised anxiety disorders and obsessive compulsive disorders) often report that they feel an intense sense of internal conflict, always on the edge, a kind of uncontrollable dread and apprehension (Kennedy 1994). They may exhibit physical reactions, such as rapid pulse, elevated blood pressure and breathing difficulties. Such individuals cannot 'snap out of it', nor can they explain why they feel this way. Such anxiety cannot be discharged by the act of the individual's will or by the reassurance of friends (Kennedy 1994).

When the person with an anxiety neurosis is an adolescent it is sometimes thought by other family members that 'anxiety and depression is normal' for this age group, but there is little basis for this view (VicHealth 1996). In fact adolescents who are under extreme stress, who experience loss, or who have learning disabilities, (e.g. dyslexia) or conduct disorders (behaviour patterns that repetitively and persistently violate the rights, privileges and privacy of others) are at a higher risk of neurotic anxiety, which may lead to depression. Adolescents who are seen as troublemakers at home, who skip school, who suffer with eating problems (serious disturbances in eating habits and appetitive behaviours) or radical changes to their diet, who have little desire for social interaction or who talk about being better off dead are in need of support and appropriate intervention. For individuals who refuse to go to school, counselling may be of some benefit. Likewise for all of the difficulties mentioned above. Quite often individuals who are exhibiting these difficulties may be suffering with deep anxiety and are not 'just being naughty' (Blagg 1987).

Meeting the challenge for neuro-typical individuals who are experiencing anxiety can vary from offering them reassurance and support to long-term psychotherapy or medication (Pringle and Thompson 1986). Pringle and Thompson suggest that the most important role for the professional is in recognising the client's anxiety state and knowing when to refer on to the GP. It is also suggested that the professional helps the anxious client deal with any social or economic concerns that may be contributing to the anxiety.

What, however, does this all mean for individuals with ASD? What if an individual cannot explain their emotional or physical experiences? What if, in fact, they are detached from such experiences because they have not been able to gather the information from their senses, experience and comprehension of such experiences? I am sure that this is true for me. This means that I and many other individuals with ASD are prone to high levels of anxiety, but cannot even express this in the way that the neuro-typically developing population can. Instead, we develop inappropriate behaviours, skin irritations, aggressiveness, paranoia, social phobias and others, inabilities to concentrate as well as the typical physical expressions that accompany anxiety.

According to Pringle and Thompson (1986) anxiety states are 'the common cold' of mental illness. They account for a large proportion of the concerns that bring clients to the doctor. For some clients their lives are dictated to by their fears and they feel unable to function. Even the smallest decision, for example, what to eat or what to wear, can seem like an impossible task. As individuals with ASD we feel this way most of the time (Lawson 1999a)!

What modes of therapy are most applicable to ASD and how can we be sure that we are providing the appropriate services and interventions? Bates (1977) suggests that the role of the professional in providing services and interventions is actually compromised due to lack of definition. Therefore, it is important to establish 'first base' with a client and not only set the ground rules but also the anticipated role of both client and worker. To do this, however, one needs to understand ASD and be fully informed of the individual's situation, personality, characteristics of anxiety and just what might be some of the ways that could be useful in reducing stress for the client.

Services and interventions

In considering the individual client the professional must decide whether the client's anxiety is socially or mentally based. For example, if a pensioner is anxious about financial commitments then their anxiety cannot be relieved with the gaining of insight! According to Erbrederis (1997), the professional should be engaged in a mental health service that seeks to restore the client to the state of 'functioning' they enjoyed before the anxiety disabled them. What, however, does this mean for individuals with ASD? How can one restore a person to an anxiety-free state if they were never there in the first place? Would it not be wiser to teach strategies that enable an individual with ASD to contain their anxiety and manage their daily life? I think that this is a better option.

Three main models for working with an anxious client

Although there may be three main models for counselling or working with individuals with anxiety, not all are suitable for individuals with ASD. A professional needs to consider the cognitive processes informing the individual's experience. When an individual is mono-tropic, inclined towards literality, does not have social priorities, finds it difficult to generalise, and so on, the psychoanalytic model might not be very effective.

THE COGNITIVE MODEL

According to cognitive theorists, neurotic anxiety results from possible dysfunctions in an individual's thinking processes. That is, 'neurotic' problems stem from illogical reasoning patterns (Herbert 1990). This theory is helpful for the professional and client because it suggests that although one may not be able to change the circum-stances or environment (e.g. the boss's attitude at work) one can take control over one's thinking about it. Ultimately this will in turn enable the client to feel less anxiety and more control in their own life (see Appendix 6).

If the professional adopted this model to help the client explore their anxiety they might use rational emotive behavioural therapy (REBT). Current studies suggest this is a very effective way of challenging thought and subsequent resultant behaviours (Engels *et al.* 1993). Therefore, it is a useful intervention strategy for some types of anxiety. I would suggest that because individuals with ASD operate at a more cognitive, rather than emotive, level, this type of intervention can be most appropriate for many of us.

THE PSYCHOANALYTIC MODEL

If the professional were to use a psychoanalytic model in counselling the client it would be because they believed the client's anxiety to be sourced in their 'unconscious'. Psychoanalysis is a set of techniques for exploring the underlying motivations of human behaviour. It might mean using the ideologies of 'free association', interpretation and transference that belong to the theory originated by Sigmund Freud. Therefore, during conversation, perhaps over many sessions, the professional would facilitate the bringing to mind of past painful encounters. In a safe, supportive environment it is hoped that as the past pain is brought to consciousness it will cease to have a fearful hold over the individual. Rather, with insight, the individual will be able to leave the experiences of the past and move on with their life (Herbert 1990). I myself underwent many years of such therapy and gained little insight or understanding of what was happening for me. I tend to think that for individuals with ASD who have huge difficulty recognising feelings and emotions, this type of intervention is unhelpful.

THE BEHAVIOUR MODIFICATION MODEL

This model suggests that abnormal behaviour is not symptomatic of underlying 'pain' in the psyche, but rather of the way a person has learnt to cope with stress, change and the challenges of the modern world (Herbert 1992). The aim of this model, in controlling anxiety, is to encourage the client to learn adaptive ways of coping with the difficulties of every day life. This can occur with specific programmes that are tailored to the particular client's needs. Usually the client's goals are mapped out along with plans on how to achieve them. For individuals with ASD, this type of intervention coupled with REBT can be most effective.

I recognise that we all experience anxiety in one form or another. In the Western world, with job uncertainty, high unemployment, divorce and longer life expectancy, neurotic anxiety and clinical depression are on the increase (Mohammad 2000). The issues for some of the world's elderly population are based around their fears concerning housing, financial security and family support. In Western society where 'independence' and 'achievement' are valued highly, the elderly citizens of society can feel useless and a burden (Blytheway 1995). This societal and individual notion of 'value' can only contribute to the growing problems of isolation, loneliness, anxiety and suicidal tendencies that exist in this group. Adults with ASD are a growing population, and one needs to consider their future from every aspect. In the past individuals were institutionalised, and this was the way such individuals saw out their days. Today, however, this rarely happens. Life skills and coping skills need to be placed on the priority list of interventions for all individuals with ASD.

Pain (1990) suggests that advocacy and raising awareness of civil and legal rights for people can be effective in preventing or compounding some of the anxiety individuals experience. Individuals with ASD also have rights but they need our support to enable action that propagates those rights! One can go on offering various treatments for mental distress and anxiety, but if we maintain the same environmental, emotional and physical triggers that facilitate anxiety, then how will we ever get off the treadmill? I think we need to consider environmental and societal shifts in our expectations of each other. We need to be more realistic, take a lifespan approach to disability and mutual ability. This could be the very paradigm that seeks to reduce anxiety and build bridges to enable the passage of a fuller life!

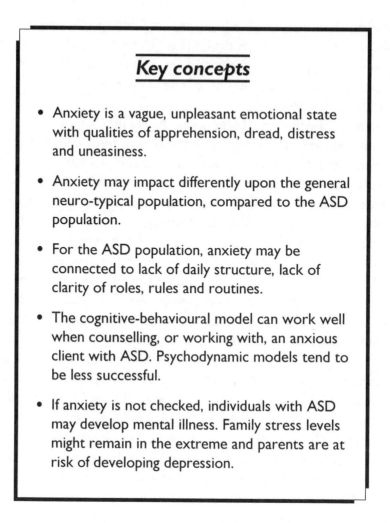

Key concepts

- Anxiety is a vague, unpleasant emotional state with qualities of apprehension, dread, distress and uneasiness.

- Anxiety may impact differently upon the general neuro-typical population, compared to the ASD population.

- For the ASD population, anxiety may be connected to lack of daily structure, lack of clarity of roles, rules and routines.

- The cognitive-behavioural model can work well when counselling, or working with, an anxious client with ASD. Psychodynamic models tend to be less successful.

- If anxiety is not checked, individuals with ASD may develop mental illness. Family stress levels might remain in the extreme and parents are at risk of developing depression.

Point to ponder

To need another person in my life shows that I am human.

CHAPTER 7

What Might it Mean to Acknowledge Difference?

Disability, different ability, or disorder?

I am not keen on the word *disorder*. It reminds me of a washing machine that is 'out of order'! However, the word *disability* has a connotation that helps me understand that I have limitations. Firstly to explore the term *disability* one might take any other 'dis' word and note the 'dis' aspects of it, for example *dis-satisfaction*. Taking this logically therefore, *dis-ability* becomes *un-ability*, just as *dis-satisfaction* becomes *un-satisfaction*. Some individuals, however, might take this a step further and believe *dis-satisfaction* to be *non-satisfaction* and *dis-ability* to be *non-ability*. To be equated with un-ability in some situations is quite different to being 'non-able'. The prefix *non* suggests a total lack of ability.

To place this further into context, picture a visually impaired individual who has their necessary aids and supports (specific prescription lenses, white cane, seeing eye dog, another individual) whilst moving around an unfamiliar supermarket. Now picture that same individual without their necessary supports moving around an unfamiliar supermarket. In one situation we would probably recognise their disability but view them as being quite able. In the other situation we might not 'see' their disability. We might perceive them as being non-able, and, as they bump into us, or other things, even see them as a being a threat to our ability!

I suggest that the very word *dis-ability* has social and medical constructs around it that need challenging. When my being autistic is seen in the context of my ability and not my dis-ability, then one is moving in the right direction. Just as when one explores the creation of a 'sighted' world or gives the visually impaired individual the means to 'see' what is around them. This implies a lack of focusing upon their 'blindness' but rather on helping them see. So it is when one adapts both the environment to fit the individual with ASD and provide them with the necessary maps for life navigation!

I would also suggest that being dis-abled is being differently able. Society would do well to accommodate and celebrate individual difference. To begin to do this, yes, one must accept dis-ability. However, in that acceptance one would benefit from understanding both the limitations and non-limitations of the individuals concerned. With the appropriate understanding, support and accommodation of such differing learning styles, the individual with ASD, and the world, can only blossom.

To view autism as a 'dis-order' is like being compared to a washing machine that is 'out of order'! To view autism as a dis-ability, within a world of neuro-typicality, should equate to un-ability in some situations, not non-ability in all! I think that even neuro-typicals find themselves dis-abled in certain unfamiliar and unrehearsed situations.

Words

Communication, orchestration and any other 'action',
Can lure and connive its path
On people's thoughts and others' behalf.
But what of us autistics?

We think and we ponder,
While you lot sit and wonder.
'What is exactly going on?'
You say within your mind.

We know without a doubt.
But you need time to work it out.
For us it's all so simple!
Words are what they seem to be.

To us there is no problem!
Herein lies the hitch you see,
Words for you or words for me?
We tend to view things differently!

(Lawson, 1998)

Any individual who is given a label that says they have a 'disorder' is going to experience 'stress'. For families with a member who has a diagnosis of ASD, this stress is enormous!

According to Sharpley and Bitsika (1999), 'the most effective means of assisting parents to deal with the day-to-day challenges they confront is to teach them ways of dealing with their children's autism-specific impairments and to help the parents themselves develop effective strategies for coping with personal stressors' (p.220). They suggest that ASD causes parents to have great concerns about their children's behaviour. Apparently, many programmes have been written to address the behavioural needs of children with ASD (e.g. applied behavioural analysis: Climas 1999), but these fail to be an effective tool for parents. I would suggest that they fail not because the programmes themselves are flawed, but because those implementing them have failed to recognise the difference between ASD cognitive processes and those of the neuro-typical world. It should also be noted that parents who experienced high levels of stress generally did not learn more effective methods for dealing with their children's needs when they participated in behaviour management training programmes (Koegel, Schreibman *et al.* 1992). The reason this was so might be that just attempting to change behaviour without understanding the purpose of that behaviour is only dealing with parts of the issue. Understanding behaviour will increase confidence and bridge the gaps in communication. Interventions can then be practised more intelligently.

Inclusive education?

Due to the very nature of ASD (being literal, monotropic, thinking in closed pictures and so on) individuals should be given the opportunity for ongoing intervention and support, if they still need it. This will have to adapt to and accommodate their growing needs as individuals and it should consider all the relevant factors: age; gender; family systems; individual personality and talents; schooling and future implications; living arrangements and future occupation; housing; personal budgeting; and peer and friendship needs.

School can be very stressful for both child and parent. Every person is an individual and no one system suits all persons. Being totally against the ideas of exclusion and separation from the hub of societal life does not automatically equate to total 'inclusion' from a mainstream school perspective. Some individuals, due to their particular needs, will always need full-time support and attention. Therefore, ideally, the education system needs to be both adaptable and considerate of individual needs. It should also be noted that even 'special schools' may be geared towards neuro-typical development of individuals with special needs and may not be ASD-aware or ASD-prepared!

Sometimes an individual with ASD can manage the school environment very well. They don't need a teacher's aide, but they still need to have their particular needs understood. Other individuals will need more support and an aide would be very helpful. In some mainstream schools a special unit is available where youngsters, particularly at secondary level, can be given extra support with social understanding and the development of social skills. It should be noted though, that because of the problems we have with generalising, social skills for the playground, the office or wherever, should not be taught in the community hall! These could simply become 'community hall skills' only. Social skills teaching needs to consider the particular settings they are for and they need to be taught 'on site'.

For other young people whose difficulties extend the usual school systems, residential schools, particularly for students with Asperger Syndrome, are proving to be successful (Scottish Society for Autism 2000). Then there are some students with ASD who are not coping well at all and who are in very fragile circumstances. These students may need home schooling. ASD is a disability within the neuro-typical world and, just as is true for many other disabilities, we need environmental, social and specific considerations that match and work with our difficulties. When this occurs many disabling situations can be turned around, and rather than feeling dis-empowered, I am empowered and enabled.

One would hope that governing bodies, be they local or national, would consider individual needs. All individuals with ASD have a right to full and complete support according to their individual needs and assessments. Parents and families with a member with ASD are usually stretched to the maximum trying to meet their family needs!

Family functioning style

Dunst, Trivette and Deal (1988) define family functioning style as 'a combination of both existing strengths and capabilities and the capacity to use these strengths to mobilise or create resources necessary to meet needs' (p.10). According to Amanda Golding, although family functioning differs for different families, coping with a child with ASD presents many very stressful challenges. It has been suggested that unsatisfactory stress levels are common occurrences for such families.

Some researchers have referred to the enriching qualities that 'disability' may have for some families. Although, as Park (1983) noted, the presence of an autistic child may actually enrich and strengthen the family unit, this response is not universal. Some parents are more likely to experience 'burnout' and eventual breakdown of the family unit (Harris and McHale 1989).

In Boyd's (1992) study of family functioning the focus was essentially upon problem solving, communication and behavioural control. Boyd found that communication was positively correlated with lowering stress, but that problem solving and behaviour control were not. Boyd's research also demonstrated that maternal stress levels were higher for families with a child with ASD than those with normal or developmentally delayed children. Boyd did not find that parents with healthy problem-solving and behavioural-control skills demonstrated lower stress levels; they were, in fact, negatively correlated. Once again this demonstrates that understanding aids communication and lowers stress, whilst behaviour interventions alone do not.

Previous research (e.g. Bristol and Schopler 1983; De Meyer 1979; Holroyd and McArthur 1976; Koegel *et al.* 1992; Perry *et al.* 1992) found that mothers of children with ASD experienced greater stress levels than controls (mothers of children with other disabilities). They also indicated that autism may be a more difficult disorder to cope with than other developmental disorders. This appeared to be due to a lack of parental confidence, as well as a lack of support and general resources. The above outcomes serve to reinforce the idea that neuro-typical cognition is not, in and of itself, enough to comprehend the world and culture of ASD. Training which is ASD specific is more useful than trying to apply neuro-typical solutions to non-neuro-typical issues.

Sharpley *et al.* (1997) found that both male and female parents of children with ASD suffered higher overall stress levels than the general population. It was also demonstrated that both male and female parents were more prone to depression than the general population. However, maternal stress was found to be higher than paternal stress levels. It was speculated that this might be connected to the fact that it was mothers who were more involved in the day-to-day care of their family member with ASD. Fathers spent longer periods away from home, either in employment or study. Therefore, one can't help but ask the question 'What effect would there be upon maternal stress levels if mothers too were able to work away from home or attend institutions of study?' Of course this would only raise other questions concerning the ability of carers to understand ASD in such places as respite care centres, kindergarten, childcare centres, schools, places of employment, and so on.

According to Beresford (1994) much research has focused on exploring the stressors associated with caring for a disabled child. However, little has been done to explore the ways that families cope. I suggest that coping with the disability of ASD, both for the individual and for the family, can only improve as understanding of both worlds is encouraged. Beresford suggests that the process model of stress and coping has shown that coping resources are interrelated and that coping resources affect the choice of coping strategy. Therefore, personal coping resources will have a direct effect upon the family's ability to find, access and utilise social support. Anxiety and stress can sap the coping resources of those amongst us with the best intentions. Stress reduction and relieving anxiety needs to happen before these personal wells of coping can be replenished.

Dyson (1993) found that parental stress and family functioning were interrelated in families with a disabled child. Stress levels were higher in such families, compared with families without a disabled child. The time factor was most significant. For example, Gallagher, Beckman and Cross (cited in Dyson 1993) found that parental stress was likely to increase with time.

According to Brinker, Seifer and Sameroff (1994) early intervention 'provided knowledge, specific suggestions for social interaction strategies, and psychological support for families of young children with developmental delays' (p.463). However, early intervention is only applicable to pre-school children. Once the children begin school intensive support might cease. It is so easy to assume that ASD children and their families only need 'extra support' whilst the children are not at school full time. In fact, the opposite may be true. Sharpley *et al.* (1997) suggest that parents of a child with ASD often feel 'unsupported, isolated and alone'. As with any other growing child, children with ASD have changing needs. Therefore, as professionals we need to look at ways of meeting these needs, rather than assuming children with ASD will outgrow the need for support.

Even within the autism continuum, children and their families have differing levels of support needs. Burke and Richdale (1997) noted that parents of a child with Asperger Syndrome (AS) suffered greater 'stress' than parents of children with Kanner's autism. This was thought to be due to the insight that AS children have that children with Kanner's autism lack. For example, AS children know they are different, but don't know how to change that and can demonstrate more difficult behaviours due to this type of frustration. In their conclusion they suggest that further research is needed to determine whether existing services, or the development of new services, could and should adequately cater for all families with children with a pervasive developmental disorder.

Individual stories and struggles

My story

AS A SMALL CHILD

Basically the world went on around me! I was scared of sudden noise, and would jump at the sound. During thunderstorms I hid under the table…and sometimes did not come out for hours. I 'played' by myself and was very content on my own. I loved the garden, as long as my younger sisters did not interrupt me. But my strongest fascination was with the sea, which was not too far away from my home.

On a couple of occasions I actually escaped from the garden and walked to the sea by myself. Its ability to woo me and draw me into itself was very strong and I had no fear at all. I was separated from the shore on one occasion and my neighbour rescued me from the incoming tide. Although my mother chastised me for 'going off' I really did not understand what all the fuss was about!

AS AN OLDER CHILD

Between the ages of five and eleven I lived very isolated from the world. My only attachments were accessed through my pets. I loved the kitten that my grandmother gave me for my fifth birthday, and he was my constant and only real companion. At school I felt confused and alone. I was constantly teased and mocked by other children. I just did not know what was going on. I did my best to please the teachers and loved to listen to the voice of one teacher in particular.

I found school rules difficult to understand and so I was often in trouble. I hated school dinners in the primary school because they usually had foods like processed peas with their fibrous hard skins and ability to pop or explode uncomfortably in my mouth, and I could not eat them.

My diet at home consisted of mashed potato, carrots and gravy! I did eat white bread and butter with various fillings (e.g. marmalade (minus the bits), jam, meat or fish paste, and cheese with tomato). The only cereal I ate was cornflakes, as long as it had the top of the milk on it (the cream), and I never ate greens, rough meat or egg whites. Textured food that was not smooth made me gag, and I felt like I would throw up if it stayed in my mouth.

For my eighth birthday I was given a new red bicycle. I loved sitting on the tarmac and spinning the wheels to watch the silver shine move with the sunlight as they went round and round. I had learnt how to ride a bike by taking my mother's bike and standing up on the pedals to propel the bike forwards. I went for many solitary rides on my bicycle. One day I was following a big red bus when it turned out on to the main road. I thought that it was OK to go because the bus went. However, I was wrong and I was knocked off my bike by a passing car coming in the other direction. They took me to hospital in the ambulance and I never saw my bike again.

When I was nearly ten I had to go to hospital for almost one year because of a bone infection in my leg. Although this was a very traumatic time it was also very stabilising because the ward routine gave me a measure of security. The thing that I hated most was waiting for visitors at visiting time, and usually no one came. I could not understand at that time how difficult it was for my mother to visit me in a hospital 14 miles away from home. Especially when she did not drive and visiting times were when my younger sisters were coming home from school. The sad thing is that no one ever talked to me or explained anything, it was just done.

For my tenth birthday the nurses brought me in a small cupcake with a large white candle in the middle. All the children sang 'Happy Birthday' and gathered around my bed. I dived under my sheet and pretended to be asleep for probably ten minutes, until they gave up and went away! I could not face them because I did not know what to do. My heart beat fast and I felt really scared so I did what I usually did and that was play 'dead' and hope it would all go away. This was a common way of coping. If I did not understand something or was not sure of how to respond, I ignored the situation. I stayed in a world of my own that I had control over, and when that failed I returned to various obsessive behaviours that gave me back a sense of connection.

TEENAGE YEARS

From age 13 to 19 I began to grasp the reality that I was different from most people around me. I found this realisation quite depressing and worked extremely hard to discover how to be like others. I had few friends that tolerated my 'strange behaviour' and when I did find a friend then I latched on to that person in an obsessive way. That person dominated my existence and it was terribly important to me that they included me in all their activities. When they did not, I became so anxious and miserable that I withdrew, sucked the roof of my mouth and rocked myself for hours.

At the age of 17 I was committed to a mental institution, labelled schizophrenic and placed on heavy medication. I remained on the medication until I was 23 years old. I have been on and off medication for years. The last antipsychotic medication (stellazine) that I took was over two years ago. I do take Zoloft, an antidepressant and a member of the SSRI (selective seretonin reuptake inhibitor) group, but am currently having a time away from this. I did find that small amounts of an SSRI help with lowering my anxiety.

ADULT LIFE

I did marry and I had four children. I am divorced now and all of my children live away from home. My youngest child, an Asperger boy of 18 years, has just passed his driving test! From what I have read I now understand so much of my life experience and I am very thankful to be free from the label of schizophrenic!

EMOTIONS

Most of my life I feel as if I am outside of what is happening around me. I rarely actually am able to identify the emotional environment of either myself or others. Life tends to be either 'happy' or 'not happy', 'angry' or 'not angry'. Until recently I always believed that if someone close to me was 'angry' then it must be because of me. Now I am beginning to realise that people can be unhappy or even angry, for many different reasons. In fact it may have nothing to do with me at all!

I think that maybe my anxiety can be so extreme because for much of the time I am excited and enthusiastic, irrespective of how others may feel, and when those emotional states are not confirmed within me by the words of others I am so lost and confused that it's terrifying. All the 'in-between' emotions on the continuum get missed. I jump from calm to panic in one major step!

BEHAVIOUR

I am much more 'in touch' with the world and 'in control' of how it affects me. This is so because I have more understanding of what is happening and I can make decisions about it. If 'things' become too much, that is I experience a kind of sensory overload, then I simply withdraw and recoup. I do not like change but sometimes changes occur when I least expect them and then I have to gather myself back again. This I do by 'self-talk' rational emotive therapy, deep breathing, and relaxation through the use of breathing. Years ago these methods were out of reach for me because I was too immature to understand them, but now I can practise them with a measure of success.

SENSATION

I appear to have very sensitive ears, eyes and skin. Certain noises very definitely 'hurt' my ears and certain lights 'hurt' my eyes. Strip lighting is one of the worst, and lights that flash. If the strip lights have a grid covering them then I cope with them better. I have an insatiable appetite for touch and love to feel the roof of my mouth, especially when I am either insecure or very secure! I love soft material and soft skin but I hate to feel my own skin against myself. This means that I need to wear pyjamas in bed or put the sheet between my legs so that they do not come into direct contact with each other.

I still jump at sudden noises and shake or flap my hands when I am excited. At times I twitch or shake involuntarily for no apparent reason. All that I can tell you is that it feels like an electric impulse passing through my body and I need to respond to it.

On campus at university studying, which I absolutely loved, when we came to the end of a semester I would sometimes walk around and around the table in the cafeteria feeling devastated because school was ending and I felt so miserable. Some of my fellow students thought that I was crying for joy because the exams were over, I told them the reason that I was upset and I think that it was quite hard for them to see my point of view!

I do not know what the future holds, but I am sure that I will continue to write and hopefully study. I would love the opportunity to share with other people some of my experiences and help to increase understanding of autism and Asperger Syndrome.

I am where I am today because certain people (and myself) believed in me. I would encourage any parent or professional not to give up on individuals with autism but to remain patient, consistent and caring. I personally believe that much can be attained with time and persistence. Growth and development take years for non-autistic people. I believe that a lot of developmental delays are happening with us, but the emphasis is upon 'delay' rather than cancellation!

I feel as if I have 'woken up' over the last ten years. It may have taken me a lot longer to grow up and I still have a long way to go, but it's pretty scary to think that I could have been closed off for ever, if certain people had not taken risks with me, or had given up on me completely!

Morgan's story – Need-based reality
(By kind permission of Morgan Allgood, USA, September 2000)

My personal reality is closer to that of my four-footed friends than it is of most people. Mine is a need-based reality. If I'm hungry, I scavenge for food in the kitchen. If I'm thirsty, I get myself something to drink. If I'm bored, or just because it's what

I do, I get on the computer. If I get bored with that, I play Tetris. If I can see a pile of laundry or a sink full of dishes, I get an inkling it needs doing and I do it.

Many of the subtler needs don't get met though, because I can't see them. I forget that I need to brush my teeth, comb my hair, change clothes. I forget that I need to take something out for dinner, or dust, or vacuum (unless, of course, there's a thorough layer of dog hair as a less than subtle clue!). Often I forget that I need to eat, because I don't feel hungry.

And planning anything is impossible. I don't plan. I just do. I do as I need. It makes writing and role play difficult. I rarely come up with an original thought of my own…except on very rare occasions when I'm having an exceptionally good day, I just follow everyone else's lead. Just the way I meander through life. No plots, no plans, just doing what's needed. No wonder the experts say we have no imagination.

It can be immensely frustrating. I love to write, but I often have to ask my husband how to structure letters to our friends on the writing list. If he doesn't tell me, it doesn't occur to me. But why would I expect any different from myself? After all, if he doesn't call to remind me to eat, it rarely occurs to me to eat lunch, or even breakfast.

But still, it is frustrating. Why can't I strategise??? Why can't I think to take care of my own less obvious needs, or tasks around the house, let alone the needs of others?

I suppose this is where people think that we are egocentric. Because our worlds revolve around immediate needs for gratification, and the inability to perceive the needs of others. But that is misleading. I do care about others, and wish I could read the signs easier and know where there is a need and how to meet it. It's a very helpless feeling, not knowing what to do for other people. But I do care.

> I feel deeply.
> I care deeply.
> I desire deeply.
> I will always tell the truth.
> That is who I am.
> I expect nothing less of you.

Mary's story
*(By kind permission of Mary Margaret Britton Yearwood,
USA, May 2000)*

High-functioning autism was rarely diagnosed when I was a child. The doctors told my mother and father I was spoiled, stubborn, rude, and lost in my own world because it was what I wanted. I would speak when I was ready. A non-verbal IQ test proved I had enough intelligence to make it in the world and convinced my parents to put me in school a year early. As far as my aversion to touch, that was growing pains, the experts assured my ever-wondering parents. 'But she isn't growing very much,' they pointed out. Growing pains were the pat answer in the 1960s to any pain doctors were not able to explain in children; therefore my extra-sensitive skin was misdiagnosed as with (I don't even want to think of how many) other children. I learned to stay away from touchy-feely humans. I learned to stay disconnected from humans in general. I found the purr and rumble of a motor more loving to my body than my mother's arms.

Today I am 36. I have been very fortunate this year. Unlike Rainman whose father left him too much money and who could make a fortune in Las Vegas, I must work to pay for my rent. This year I found a work that seems to fit me. I am a chaplain to persons with Alzheimer's. I see through my neurological difficulties into theirs and pray I bring them a little bit of comfort. I consider myself lucky for finding a work that fits me. But this does not discount my lonely childhood and my ongoing pain of trying to make it in a world I do not understand.

'My Shoes' is a story about my thinking that my clothing was a part of my skin and not an item to be discarded. And I didn't 'play' in my shoes; I lived wholeheartedly and I was trapped in my own world, not by choice as persons think when they think of play. I was an explorer and a pirate and all the other things described in this next piece.

Shoes

I have a pair of slip-on sneakers that I don't have to tie.
The Mama says they are old and dirty and we need
to throw them away.
'No' I say.
On Sunday we go to picnic in the park with the hippies.
My parents are older than the hippies but they are
actors and they like the hippies.
The Mama has long beautiful hair that hangs all the
way to her bottom.
The Daddy has hair down to his shoulders.
They look like the hippies.
They stopped and got a bucket of chicken from the colonel.
I do not like fried chicken. I do not want to eat a bird.
Birds are my friends.
I eat potato salad instead.
My boy is 11 and he likes chicken very much.
My baby is 3 and she likes chicken very much.
I am the only one who does not like chicken.
It is so hot that we take off our shoes. We run to the playground
and the grownups watch from far away.
I swing and I slide. There is a slide that has a tunnel on it.
For a long time you can disappear
from the grownups.
I am an army soldier fighting in a war. I parachute
down the slide to save my country.
I shimmy up one of the tall poles on the swing set. I am an explorer.
I am the first girl to climb to the North Pole. I can
see the whole world from up here.
The grownups say it is time to go.
We climb in the old station wagon. Me, my baby, and my
boy climb in the back seat.
I feel so free and happy from discovering the North Pole
and from saving my country from enemies.

We are leaving the park and I look at my feet. 'MY SHOES!'
I shriek. 'MY SHOES, MY SHOES.'
'Should we go back?' The Daddy asks the Mama.
'NO!' says the Mama. 'We will not go back
and get those horrible shoes.
Sharon Margaret it is time to get a new pair of shoes.'
It is no use. They are from another planet. They do not understand.
I jump in the 'way back' of the station wagon
and look desperately out the back window.
I can still see the picnic table where my shoes are
still sitting nicely where I put them.
They are waiting for me to come back and get them.
'Someone will steal my shoes.' I yell to the people
in the front of the car.
The mama says, 'Your shoes will be placed in the
garbage where they belong.'
I can't see the picnic table anymore.
I curl up in a ball so far away from the grownups.
No one can get me now.
I cry, 'My shoes, my shoes, my magic shoes.'
I think, How will I be able to leap tall buildings?
How will I be able to defend my country from the enemy?
How will I fight dragons and monsters and sharks?
How will I get to the North Pole?
Oh my shoes. The little girl in red needs her shoes.
Rock the little girl in red. Keep her in a ball.
Don't let them touch you.
People hurt.
People hurt.
Oh god I want my shoes.
I need my shoes. They are mine.
They are magic.
Doesn't anyone understand? I want my shoes.
Those shoes have
killed millions of dragons, climbed millions of mountains,

gone back in time to a million places.
Those shoes have outrun polar bears and cobras and tigers.
Those shoes are a part of me.
Don't you see?
That is me on that table in the park.
That is me!
That is me!

Wild Kittens

My grandma has wild kittens
in the old shack next to her house.
I watch her put the left over lunch
into the chipped porcelain pan.
She mixes
in dry cat food, dry milk and rusty water.
My grandma doesn't talk
for this is an important job that takes
a lot of concentration.
My grandma always does
important things like
feeding wild kittens and burning the trash.
She carries the cat feast out the back screen door.
The door squeaks at her. I follow my grandma
but she waves at me to stay back.
Wild kittens don't like little girls, not even little girls in red.
Wild kittens only like my grandma.
I sit on the cold concrete steps.
My grandma crosses the yard and she disappears into
the shack that the grown-ups call The Old Kitchen.
I see big cats race across the yard as my grandma talks in cat talk.
Cat talk sounds like this: Here kitty, kitty.
In cat talk, here kitty kitty means I love you.
I don't see any wild kittens but I know they are there.

My boy told me so and my boy doesn't lie about
important things like kittens.
I am tired of sitting on the steps, so I hide under the
house and sit in the cool black dirt.
I am a wild kitten.
My grandma can't see me, but she knows that I am here.

The Future

Life on earth is but a moment caught within the crease of
time,
The seasons come and go again,
You have your life, and I have mine.
The seed that's planted within the ground
Cannot choose what to become.
A potato, an apple or a rose for some.

However, for it to be the very best,
It needs rich soil, not poor.
The sun and the rains must come,
To open that seed's door.

I may be born to nourish others,
I may delight the senses.
I may grow tall,
I may grow small,
I may stay stunted beneath wire fences.

My future may not depend on my stock,
So much as it does upon sources.
Sources of warmth, sources of care
I depend on the nurture to be for me there.

Then I can blossom and sing with the birds,
Then I can grow my potential.
So plant me in goodness and all that is fine,
Please keep the intruders away.
Give me a chance to develop, in time,
To become who I am, in life's future, one day!

(Lawson, 1999)

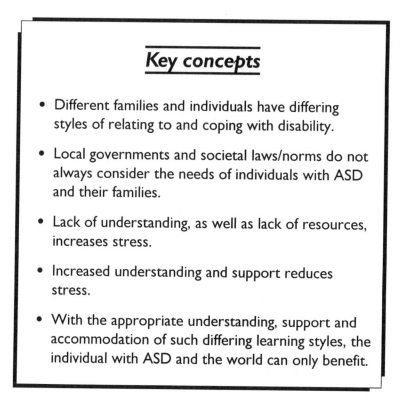

Key concepts

- Different families and individuals have differing styles of relating to and coping with disability.

- Local governments and societal laws/norms do not always consider the needs of individuals with ASD and their families.

- Lack of understanding, as well as lack of resources, increases stress.

- Increased understanding and support reduces stress.

- With the appropriate understanding, support and accommodation of such differing learning styles, the individual with ASD and the world can only benefit.

Point to ponder

How can I be a part of the solution, rather than the problem?

PART III

Ideas for Action

CHAPTER 8

Practical Implications
and Interventions

Management techniques

According to the *Oxford English Dictionary* to manage something or someone means to be able to 'have effective control of, bend to one's will, cajole…bring about, secure, deal with or handle with skill…'. This could be interpreted to mean that any strategy that can be used successfully to enable a situation or behaviour to be controlled, managed, used profitably or contained, to produce the desired response, results or profit, (for the owner of such management), might be useful. However, for our purposes 'handle with skill' will be the preferred definition. This implies appropriate management that both respects the client, having their needs uppermost in mind, and fosters an atmosphere of cooperation leading to desired outcomes.

It is important to remember that individuals with ASD are generally monotropic. They are better at doing one thing at a time, as opposed to several things at once. This will mean that the parent or teacher needs to prioritise the issues that they want to pursue or follow up with an individual with ASD. All communication needs to be clear, and one needs to check in on just what has been understood. For example, working on a child's ability to sit relatively still at 'mat time' might be the first issue to deal with, rather than their lack of being attentive. It may be assumed that a child understands that *sitting* on the mat at mat time means that she or he has to *sit still* on the mat with the other children. However, an ASD child may not in fact understand this. Due to having a diminished sense of 'other' they may not know that they are included in the general concept or instruction. ASD children need, therefore, to be given clear instruction about any activity. This may need to be given in pictorial form and in stepped out sequences, as a social story (see Chapter 10).

To make plans and to plot to 'upset the other children' or any other person requires considerable ability at scheming and at being able to organise and recognise 'outcomes'. This requires a well-developed sense of 'other'. This is unlikely to be true for a child with ASD. It is more likely that individuals with ASD haven't any idea of how their behaviour impacts upon others. This is something that we would need to be taught over time. This can be done via social story and role-play.

It is often said that a child will eat when hungry. This may not be the case for children with ASD. Recognising hunger means being able to connect with the bodily discomfort of hunger and interpret it as such. For some children with ASD this connection appears to be lacking. Having specific rules that the child eats at breakfast time, lunchtime and dinnertime, might be helpful. Using a motivator (e.g. special time to do their obsession or enjoy a particular event), can be offered as a reward for eating. Food may need to be offered with limited fuss, in limited amounts and in a particular form that the child finds palatable. All nutritional programmes should be guided by the expertise of a paediatrician.

For aggressive outbursts (often used because alternative ways of letting others know how we feel, haven't been taught) demonstrate and teach (via pictures, cartoons and/or comic strip stories) no kicking, biting, punching, etc., BUT you can let others know what is happening for you by:

- using a mood clock (see p.137 for how to make a 'mood' clock)

- placing an object in a situation that is not usual for that object to tell others that you aren't coping (e.g. putting a pencil in the fruit bowl, or a banana in the pen jar, to indicate to others that you are beginning to feel overwhelmed and need space or some time to process).

Some individuals with ASD find it helpful to listen to soothing music (the definition of soothing is different for different people) through headphones. Music can be a useful anti-stressor. Some individuals with ASD need open space; lots of walking can be helpful as an anti-stressor. Some need to spin, flap, cut or tear paper (keep paper allowed for cutting in a particular container only for such paper) and should be allowed to do so in an ordered, structured environment for a fixed amount of time only. There probably are other useful things that aid stress reduction and sensory reduction. I think it is important to be clear with instructions, be consistent and concise. It is also important not to be too demanding and to remember individuals with ASD are usually monotropic and prefer to do things one at a time, rather than several things at once.

The following may also be helpful with aggressive or antisocial behaviours.

Hitting, either adults or children:

(a) maintain arm's length where possible

(b) verbally 'hands down' – conversational tone

(c) physically direct arms down

(d) redirect to task.

Kicking, strategy for adults or children:

(a) endeavour to be at side during all activities (not in front of)

(b) ignore

(c) re-direct to current activity.

Stripping off:

(a) retrieve clothes

(b) give clothes to child to dress themselves with supervision.

Throwing self on to floor:

(a) ignore for 30 seconds – say nothing during this period

(b) 'stand up'

(c) then redirect.

Head butting:

(a) always work from the side to avoid being butted by child's head

(b) if child tries to butt, ignore and move away

(c) return to work with the child after 30 seconds and encourage child to finish task

(d) re-direct if necessary

(e) give praise appropriately.

Trashing room:

(a) verbal reprimand instantly 'No…' (define what it is); repeat twice

(b) protect others

(c) say 'Leave room please'

(d) ignore

(e) invite back to room after enough 'cooling off' time has passed

(f) if individual says 'No', ignore, and move away

(g) repeat instruction after 60 seconds.

The above strategies are directed at behaviour *only* and do not attempt to understand 'why' the individual does what they do. However, it is important to recognise that all behaviour is functional. Understanding this is vital. I know we need to protect the individual and those around them, so demonstrating appropriate behaviour is the best way to do this. When the individual's behaviour is appropriately reinforced then they are being given alternative communication skills, hopefully, and are learning that to scream, hit, bash, strip off, throw oneself on the ground or trash a room, is not the way to express discomfort, unhappiness, insecurity, or fear. The individual, therefore, needs to be encouraged to express their unhappiness differently. For example, being given a photo of an 'unhappy' face, preferably the individual's own, and encouraged to show this picture instead of screaming, or producing other inappropriate responses.

If the individual is non-verbal, the use of pictures, colours and actions, demonstrated by the parent, teacher or professional, can be most helpful. However, this needs to be done when the individual is cooperative and willing. Even when an individual is verbal, colours, symbols, signs and actions might be useful. This is so because even though the individual with autism may 'feel' unhappy, they may not have the skills or comprehension to know what the feeling is.

Anger Management

Being angry is probably an emotion that most of us will experience at one time or another. Is it OK to be angry? Yes, it is! However, how many of us know how to deal with our anger and use it constructively? Anger can be one of the most damaging emotions known to humankind. A sense of injustice is something most of us will identify with at some level or other. Do we turn this experience into internalised anger and harm ourselves? By this I mean that if someone does an injustice to me and I become bitter about it, who gets hurt? I suggest to you that, in fact, I am hurting only myself. So often, the recipient of my anger is totally unaware of how or why I feel the way I do! For many individuals with ASD, injustice, as they perceive it, has to be expressed. Sometimes they move into self-injury, at other times they verbally or physically attack others.

As we agree that it is OK to feel angry, what do we do about expressing it? For individuals with ASD we often do this without being aware of 'appropriate anger expression'. The following are a few ideas that might be helpful.

MOOD CLOCK

Materials

- One cardboard/paper barbecue plate.
- Five broad colouring pens of differing colours
- One gold or silver split pin
- One piece of card (4 inches long) to make a pointer from

Method

With the teenager or young person create a list of expressions, e.g. feeling very angry; leave me alone; approach with caution; enter at own risk; ready to talk.

Allow the individual to colour triangular sections on the barbecue plate and place each separate expression into one coloured section. The split pin is to be pushed through the centre of the plate holding the cardboard pointer and allowing it to be moved freely.

The young person is instructed that they are allowed to feel angry or upset but they are not allowed to injure themselves or others, or damage property. Instead the mood clock can be placed on the refrigerator door with fridge magnets and act as a useful tool that enables them to communicate to others how they feel.

TRAFFIC LIGHT CARDS

Rationale

Individuals with ASD have the right to know and understand their environment. When you have problems with predicting outcomes, manipulation of others, as well as the environment, can mean forming rules, rituals and repetitive behaviours. If we do not give individuals with ASD the tools to choose to act, then we limit their choices. Without knowledge and 'know-how' individuals usually resort to 'reaction'. The following method is a way of providing further appropriate tools to enable individuals to choose to act.

Materials

- A3 sheets of card
- Red, green and orange marker pens
- Black writing pen
- Hole punch
- Key ring
- Ability to laminate cards and thread on to key ring, if desired

Method

Draw up separate playing size cards on the A3 sheets. Colour in red, amber and green traffic lights on the front side of each card.

On the flip side of the card write down an alternative action for the individual that will mean an alternative to kicking, biting, punching, and so on. For example, if a child is feeling uncomfortable or is being bullied in the playground at school: Go to library and sit on your green bean bag. The on-duty library teacher would need to know the individual has such cards acting as a prompt to support them. The teacher would also need to understand the implications for the individual concerned and be prepared to offer assistance.

For use at home, the child can be taught to locate their card/s either in their pocket or on their key ring. The cards act as a prompt to offering an alternative response (appropriately discussed and formulated through conversation with parent/carer and the individual concerned) enabling the individual to choose a positive action as opposed to a reaction of aggression or self-abuse.

The alternative responses must be discussed with the individual to make sure they are agreeable to him or her. When individuals are non-verbal or do not read, then a pictorial representation can be used. Some individuals respond well to instruction that is given in comic strip form using their favourite cartoon characters.

DEMONSTRATING THE DIFFERENCES BETWEEN 'ON PURPOSE' AND 'ACCIDENTAL'

Rationale

Many young people with ASD find it difficult to tell the difference between actions that are accidental and those that spring from deliberate motivation. What is the difference between reality and fantasy? How can one tell the difference between a thought, an idea and a wish? (Centuries of philosophers have debated this!) The following is a sample role play that attempts to illustrate 'accidental' and 'on purpose'.

Materials

- Two chairs
- Two neuro-typicals and one individual with ASD

Method

Please note: This exercise can be a classroom project along with others that demonstrate abstract concepts such as: up, under, over, through, fantasy, imagine, real, true and false, etc. This is important because it is wise not to separate out the child with ASD as being the only one in need of such helpful explanations!

Explain to the two individuals with neuro-typicality that they will be sitting on a chair quite close to each other. Another individual (with ASD) will pass between the chairs and will (because the chairs are so close) inevitably touch the individuals sitting on the chairs. The children are scripted to announce 'You knocked me', to which the individual with ASD may reply 'I couldn't help it. You were in my way'. The teacher can then explain that the action was 'an accident' and was not born from a deliberate intention to 'hurt' or 'knock' the person who was passing between the two chairs.

Timetables

When planning a timetabled event, allow for another timetabled event to take place if the regular event has to be cancelled. It is actually beneficial to allow for three timetabled events to be displayed with a tick against that which will happen and a cross against those, which will not. For example: Swimming is set for period 1, teacher gets sick, swimming is cancelled. Event 2, indoor sports, will take place instead, perhaps with an agency relief teacher. Event 1 (swimming) and Event 3 (show and tell) will have an X by them, showing cancelled.

Monday	Tuesday	Wednesday	Thursday	Friday
Swimming	Music	History	Mathematics	English
Indoor Sports	Team Sports	Art	Computer	Literacy
Show and tell	Story time	Pottery	Academics	Reading
A tick can be placed against the event that is expected to occur ✓				
A red cross can be placed over the event that is not going to take place ✗				

The escaper

Kate Rankin (1992) reveals in the story concerning her son that escaping from the house was 'one of Gabriel's strongest aims in life'. Kate goes on to say that absolutely nothing could deter her son from escaping. This appears to be the case for so many children with autism (Asperger Syndrome Parents Group 1996). The only kinds of management appear to be those directed at implementing the child's safety. For example, 'extreme vigilance, the locking of all doors and windows, knowing the whereabouts of the child at all times and even resorting to the wearing of a bell or alarm if the child should stray beyond a certain point' (Rankin 1992). Kate even suggests (for those who could afford it!) closed circuit TV, buzzers on doors, windows and gates, and a permanently manned watchtower in the garden!!

On a more serious note (although Kate does have a point) Attwood (1992) suggests that some 'autistic' behaviours are signs of stress and expressions for 'help'. For example: a child may bite their hand when they have failed to complete a task and need help. Attwood suggests the following:

- identify any signals which indicate increased levels of stress

- organise some distracting activity

- encourage relaxation or vigorous physical activities to reduce the stress level

- impose verbal control

- leave well alone.

Suggestions for the ASD youngster obsessed with chasing cars

Need to find a strong motivator that will encourage him or her not to chase cars. For example, each time he or she chooses not to chase a car there is a reward that is the motivation to stop. This might be something like time on the computer; time with another of his 'more acceptable' obsessions; anything that is seen by him as a terrific thing, that is permissible and OK by parents. Avoid food rewards unless they are healthy, e.g. apple juice; McDonald's (kidding). No, really my son was into star charts. When he had enough stars I bought him a game for his Nintendo.

This elimination practice might be a good way to go. Rather than saying 'No' to running after cars at all, the child might be allowed to run along the length of three houses, then two and one until none is achieved. Rewards need to be instant, and no attention given when instruction is broken. There must always be the rule though, that he or she NEVER goes on to the road, unless crossing it when instructed to do so. This rule is not negotiable!

Sleeping problems

Anyone could have an unusual sleeping pattern; it is interesting to note though that sleeping difficulties are very common in autism. I tend to need less sleep than my neuro-typical friends. I have problems getting off to sleep and problems staying asleep! In fact, if I have four hours sleep during a night, I am doing well! A few of my friends say that their autistic child is a terrific sleeper…never any worries in that department. Well, that's great. But, I seem to hear more stories from parents that have children who don't find sleeping an easy pastime. This can be hard on everyone.

I find it worthwhile having a few rules…like, 'I know I shouldn't wake anyone else up who is still sleeping'. (I used to make lots of noise and then when someone came to investigate I would say 'Oh, you are finished sleeping now so I'll come and wake you up!') I don't do that now! I just have a list of things that I can amuse myself with then, when it's morning (not before 6am) I can wake them with a cup of tea. I'm not allowed to talk to them about 'Wendy's stuff' though, not until after breakfast!

It's OK not to sleep, especially when you are not tired, but when you are tired and you can't sleep…but you wish you could…that's horrid!

Coping with stress

It is usual that individuals with autism will have a pattern of communicating stress. It may be certain sounds, movements or phrases that they associate with the situation, even if the words they use are reintroduced from some previous time (Attwood 1992). Once signals are understood, distraction may help. If this does not occur then relaxation with soothing music or other calming remedies may help. Some children need to 'burn off' their energy before they can calm down. If seclusion is necessary for the person to feel safe and separated from what was upsetting them, then make sure that the area is comfortable.

Sometimes relaxation can involve breathing calmly and deeply in a controlled manner. Children can be taught a breathing technique but it takes persistence and patience (Attwood 1992). At other times verbal control is vital for the child to know that even if they feel out of control YOU are not! Being assertive and 'applying the brakes' is just another way of setting boundaries. Should none of the above management skills be effective, then maybe the child needs to be left alone for a short period of time in a safe place. This may not mean removing oneself too far from the person but far enough so that the individual feels that they have space and privacy to work things out.

Powell and Jordan (1992) suggest that individuals with autism can have their thinking remediated. According to them, since individuals with autism can only concentrate on one thing at a time, rather than filtering out all other stimuli which may interfere with the learning of a procedure or command, a way has to be found to help maintain their focus so that they learn how not to switch channels to a distracting stimulus. This can be achieved in various ways:

- Facilitating an appropriate learning medium that takes into account any other social/affective stimuli that may be occurring simultaneously. It is not sensible to try to teach something when other things are happening.

- Attending to meaning or selective attention which is profitable to the learning process.

- Visual mediation such as photographs, plans or outlines, which can help a person with autism make appropriate decisions and interpretations. It must be taken into account that for the person with autism to make a simple choice is most difficult.

I have noted that when I am using a particular channel to address a task, if I attempt to introduce another channel, then I lose my place in the completion of that task and need to begin again. This is very frustrating! For example, you might notice that when a child with ASD is using the channel of 'touch' to dress themselves, if an adult then says 'look at what you are doing' (introducing a second channel, vision) the child may stop the task altogether and react with aggression, self-injury or by giving up on the task completely.

Abnormal posture

Kohen-Raz, Volkmar and Cohen (1992) suggest that some of the abnormal postures of individuals with ASD may be connected with 'stress' or with hypersensitivity to vestibular irritation. They also state that the pattern of lateral sway in low-functioning autistic children may be the result of general postural immaturity. If this is the case, then exercises for motor control, similar to those practised in kindergarten and primary school, could be helpful. Some research shows that when regular exercise is undertaken learning is also enhanced in academic ways (Sharpe and Ross 1987).

Natural language and motivators

Koegel, Koegel and Surratt (1992) found that incorporating parameters of natural language interactions (talking naturally) and motivational techniques (rewarding) in autistic children with severe disabilities, reduced the number of disrupted behaviours. They suggest that results were higher when persons were naturally reinforced during ordinary conversation as they made attempts at communication. The traditional analogue clinical format was not so successful during teaching sessions and more disrupted behaviours were noted.

This, therefore, suggests that even non-verbal autistic children can respond better to learning situations when they are part of natural two-way communication with motivational reinforcement. I know that, for me, I always knew if the person speaking to me valued me as another human being, or 'looked down' on me. If I felt respected and important then I also respected the individual who was interacting with me.

Personal hygiene

A number of 'toileting programmes' exist to aid the process of teaching toileting to youngsters with ASD. There isn't enough space here to explore them all. Local ASD support associations are a great contact for these programmes. The main issues to consider are that a child may not be connecting with what has to happen. The steps for toileting can be given via a social story using lots of visual aids and supports. Even the 'dog turd' bought from the joke shop can be an effective implement to demonstrate where 'the poo' goes!

Bladder control

Richdale and Prior (1992) noted that in children with high-functioning autism, poor bladder control during the day, for children integrated into the normal school system, was related to stress. They found that the high-functioning autistic children in their sample had no evidence of abnormal urinary cortisol circadian rhythm but were subject to greater 'stress' reaction than non-autistic children.

This problem therefore, needs to be managed with 'stress' relief and should be explored on an individual basis.

Attentional deficits

Wainwright-Sharp and Bryson (1993) found that individuals with ASD have problems with registering, processing and responding to external stimuli. Their research supports previous findings that 'attentional dysfunction underlies autistic symptomatology' (e.g. Bryson, Wainwright-Sharp and Smith 1990; Dawson and Lewy, 1989). This would suggest that the giving of information, instructions or relating conversationally, needs to be done simply, repetitively and in small bursts. Otherwise the person with autism may be left at the gate while the other has crossed the road.

Tantam, Holmes and Cordess (1993) also noted that attention deficit was evidenced in persons with autism. They suggest that social attention deficits are a result of neuro-physiological abnormality. More recently, Graves and Bartak (1999) have noted the coexistence of disorders of attention and disorders of the autism spectrum. They state: 'As a principle of developmental disabilities, multiple impairments are the rule rather than the exception.' However, when one considers the notion of monotropism and expert focusing, one might conclude that the issue is not one of attention deficit but rather one of attentional difference! I think that this is much more the case.

Strategies to help with rejection and failure

It's good to remember that although life is full of rejection, failure and disappointment, it is also full of acceptance, success and achievement. I think that it is important to put the things that don't work out for us, into an overall perspective. I know for myself, it is much easier to focus on my 'lack' of skills, 'lack' of successes and 'lack' of friends! I am sure that I have succeeded at a number of things, but when I am feeling like everything I touch goes wrong, the things that have worked seem far away!

Therefore, for myself I aim to have a balanced perspective on life. It's OK to fail, it's OK to be rejected, and it's OK to have fewer friends than I wish I had. Failing at things doesn't mean that I am a failure. It just means that I will not succeed at everything and not every one will love me.

In an ideal world children need to fail and they need to know that this is OK. What actually happens though, is that they only get rewarded when they do what is right or when they act appropriately. Very few adults actually say to young people 'It's OK, you got it wrong this time, but it's OK, you are OK'. This type of conversation needs to happen often in the world of ASD. We are so monotropic that we only focus in on one thing at one time. This is usually failure! Helping us to focus in on the successes would be more helpful, at these times.

Perhaps organising for us to list all the things we are good at, all the things we would like to do, or all the things we would like to see happen or experience might be beneficial. Set some very achievable goals for us, so that we won't fail at these. Then move us on to slightly bigger goals...ones we have to work towards. Ultimately, we need some long-term goals that the other goals can be working towards. At first we will need to experience immediate rewards. We are not good at postponing gratification. Then we can have rewards that take a bit longer to get, and so on. When a person with ASD is so focused, there can be no other way. We are not good at understanding that there are alternatives! We need help here.

Sometimes comic strip stories can be useful, as can types of social stories that take us through life encounters using our favorite heroes (The Simpsons, *Star Trek* characters, etc.). Sometimes visual clues given as you speak (pictures/photos or guided wording with activity) that take us away from failure towards success. For example, don't call us 'silly duffer' when we mess up, but do say 'Oh well, we all make mistakes, it's OK…come over here and let's…'. This moves a person on to what they can do and can do well. It also gives you a chance to applaud their success and refocuses them on to a more positive note.

At times, when dealing with teens and young adults who have little self-esteem, it can be very hard to undo what has taken them years of 'failure' to build! You need to tread slowly and carefully. Possibly a 'peer' support person might be useful. Someone who the young person can identify a bit with but doesn't feel threatened by. The peer support person will need to understand ASD and must be willing to be committed to the friendship. Clear friendship lines need to be established, for example: a) when the friend is contactable and when not; b) what they are happy to do, where they can go and what time they can give; and c) what they can do when things are not going well (so they don't just drop out of the picture). If the peer support person isn't taken care of and they become unsure of their role, they will quickly 'burn' out and become one more 'failure' to add to our list.

I'm sure there are many more positive ways to encounter 'failure' and help to re-establish self-esteem. Happy hunting!

Handling change

> '*My son has a great love for keeping things in specific order, especially in his room. If things get messed up, or changed he reacts angrily and will sometimes hit out at me. Any ideas for helping him keep calm and fix the things up without there being too much frustration?*'

First, it's important to remember that we are very good at many things. Especially those things requiring structure, format, attention to detail, order and sameness. However, for many of us 'change' can be very uncomfortable. To recapitulate, I think this is because:

- Most of us are probably designed to be monotropic. We are not good at thinking, doing or being more than one thing at one time. For example, we look or listen, not keen on doing both together. We focus on detail, not good at seeing the whole picture.

○ We find it hard to predict consequences. This means we are not good at probabilities or clues that lead to forming an appropriate conclusion.

○ We tend to think in closed frames (pictures, scenarios, concepts), and because each is different we find it hard to generalise.

If you think about life from our perspective, therefore, you can imagine why change can be so difficult for many individuals with ASD. There are some things that might help though. I think the following could be useful:

○ Work with us to *design a system* that works for us both. For example, colour coding, numbering, naming or sorting by some means according to types, products, placing, belongings, time of day, and so on. Having a system for a variety of projects is very useful. This will let us each know where something 'fits' and will assist in knowing where to place displaced items. It also decreases panic and stress when we are confronted with change.

○ Tell us '*social stories*' that use intent, context and scale. We often miss these things and so find it hard to 'read' others. Helping us to plan for everyday events can assist us in knowing what to do, what to expect and when to expect it.

○ Explain the *rules and processes* to us that are used in our home or in the dwellings of others. We will not usually automatically know these things. Even if we know the rule for one event, it doesn't necessarily mean we will know it for another, however similar.

○ Using photos or other *visual cues* may be helpful. We tend to understand better when we can 'see' the process.

○ Please avoid just changing things without letting us know about it. Sudden change is very threatening, and yes, we will act with disappointment and even aggression. We feel violated. If you cannot *prepare us in advance* (minutes will do) then social stories about 'unexpected change' are helpful. Having a distracter can also be useful. For example, a special toy, place, or activity only accessed when sudden change occurs.

Sibling support

The practical aspects involved with organising and facilitating a sibling support group are:

- contact person and facilitators
- venue, date and time
- advertising
- age groups
- activities, interaction and follow-up.

1. Prepare a programme.

2. Have a facilitator or appropriate adult in charge, for each small group of between 4–6 children.

3. Have separate rooms for each group.

4. Meet each child, give out expected programme (any indemnity forms to sign or receipts to parents).

5. Have ground rules (mutual respect, no going outside or away from room without permission, turn taking, listening, etc.).

6. Each child to get a coloured sticker to say their name and group they belong to.

7. Nibbles and drinks provided at recess time or at facilitator's discretion.

Group activities for children aged 7–12

Whilst one age group plays games or some form of team sport, another group (maximum of four groups) can be with the counsellor engaged in time for discussion of specific issues triggered via the crossword challenge (p.149), story examples, role plays, show-and-tell activity and other introductory material. After an hour the groups swap over.

Listening

It is important to have an adult 'in charge' at all times. It is also important to listen to each child or young person, so that they feel 'heard' and understood. If it appears that the child is 'at risk' (depression, suicide) then ongoing counselling support needs to be available.

All discussion is confidential and parents need to be informed that conversations with their child will not be discussed with them. If, however, a child is at risk, then the child will be informed that their parents will be told and will be given information to aid support.

Continuity

It is important that any sibling group be given continuity and not be seen as a one-off or infrequent meeting. Meetings need to be regular, ongoing and structured to take into account the growing needs of the group members. Sometimes pen pals or peer support can grow from the group meetings.

Crossword challenge

As young people explore the answers on their crossword puzzle, much debate and discussion can be generated. For example: 'What does it mean to be a member of a team?' 'Is a family like a team?' 'My brother/sister doesn't pull his/her weight in the family. I feel that my life is unfair,' 'Am I allowed individual emotions?' 'I want to cry when my autistic brother/sister breaks or misuses my things. My parents say I need to be more patient,' 'Why does he/she get away with everything?'

Being given a forum to own and express their feelings is vital for the development of healthy attitudes. Helping the sibling to explore ways they might effectively deal with what they feel and even look at practical remedies (locks on one's door) is important.

SIBLING ACTIVITY SHEET

THE CROSSWORD CHALLENGE

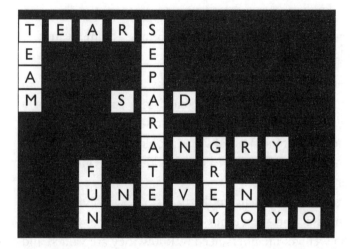

Down

1 Often needed in sports

2 I am an individual

3 Sometimes life feels this colour

4 Sometimes I want some

5 The opposite to yes

Across

1 Salt water melts in my eyes

2 Opposite to glad

3 I often see red

4 Like a bumpy road

5 Goes up and down

After some discussion time (30 minutes) the group is asked to complete some other challenges. It is hoped that these tasks will encourage thought and positively aid the individuals in their own family journey.

Other challenges

a) Write a story about your ideal family

b) How would you survive in a desert? Out of the following four items, choose the two most important – knife, water, map, blanket.

The appropriate answer is a map and some water. The group then discusses how these tools could be likened to a survival kit for a healthy family. For example, having a 'map' of family goals is useful in the navigation of potential pitfalls and problems. Taking the time to 'nurture' oneself (water) helps to prevent 'the grass on the other side is greener' syndrome!

There is a tendency to focus on the needs of the individual with ASD. This is natural and sometimes necessary. However, for family life to function well, all members need to know they are valued and valuable contributors. Siblings don't need any extra 'burdens'. It's hard enough being a member of any family, let alone one that offers a harbour for autism spectrum disorder. Please don't take this negatively. As a person with ASD, I know how difficult it can be for others to understand and perceive my difference in a positive way. I encourage readers to think of ASD as 'a differing learning style', rather than a disorder. However, in a neuro-typical world I recognise I have a disability which could cause conflict; therefore, measures that aid stress reduction for us all are important.

For teens and older individuals

Support and self-help groups can be a useful tool for any age sibling of an individual with ASD. Examples and activities for such groups are outside the scope of this book. However, it just takes a few keen people, some time, commitment and a venue and these things can be gainfully explored.

This chapter only touches the edges of many questions and concerns that individuals have when living or working with us as people with an autism spectrum delay. This book cannot address them all. However, I hope that the ideas expressed will at least promote creative thinking and more informed understanding so that many more issues can be considered with confidence.

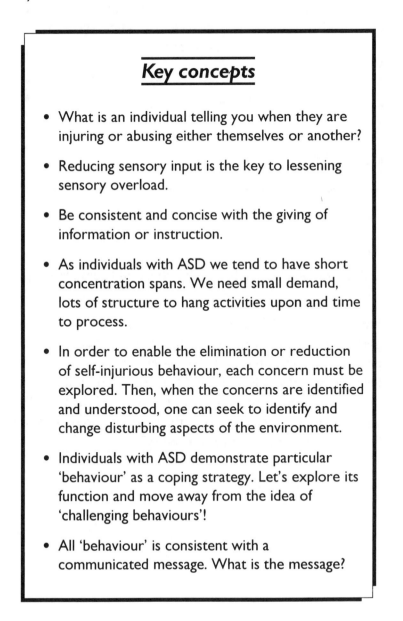

Key concepts

- What is an individual telling you when they are injuring or abusing either themselves or another?

- Reducing sensory input is the key to lessening sensory overload.

- Be consistent and concise with the giving of information or instruction.

- As individuals with ASD we tend to have short concentration spans. We need small demand, lots of structure to hang activities upon and time to process.

- In order to enable the elimination or reduction of self-injurious behaviour, each concern must be explored. Then, when the concerns are identified and understood, one can seek to identify and change disturbing aspects of the environment.

- Individuals with ASD demonstrate particular 'behaviour' as a coping strategy. Let's explore its function and move away from the idea of 'challenging behaviours'!

- All 'behaviour' is consistent with a communicated message. What is the message?

- When working with specific issues, remember to prioritise and only work with one issue at one time.

- Incorporating parameters of natural language interactions and motivational techniques, in autistic children with severe disabilities, reduces the number of disruptive behaviours.

- As individuals with ASD we need to 'experience' our learning. Finding ways to connect us to events, issues, emotions and processes is an important part of increasing and fulfilling our potential.

Points to ponder

- Self-injury can also result from boredom, ill health, anxiety and habit!

- Individuals with ASD need choices to be limited and not overpowering. For example: A choice of a savoury sandwich or a honey sandwich is probably easier to make than deciding between honey and jam! Rather than ask a child if they would like an ice-cream (knowing what one means by the term 'like' which is quite abstract, can be difficult to interpret), try saying '...ice-cream...chocolate or strawberry?'

CHAPTER 9

Social Understanding

Nurturing self-esteem

Having a healthy sense of self, or a high self-esteem, depends upon many factors. A self-concept grows from the benefits of experience, as a result of personality attributes as well as a result of upbringing. It may not be possible to change one's personality very much, but one can challenge one's thinking.

Creating the right environment for plants to grow is a fact that so many of us take for granted. Self-esteem is a bit like a plant. It needs nourishing and nurturing for it to develop in a healthy way. The way we speak to each other can be helpful, or not so helpful!

Preparing a social skills programme can be one way of instilling confidence into individuals with ASD. Giving them the skills to interact with others, express their concerns appropriately and share their experiences, is a terrific self-esteem booster.

Social skills programme

AIM

- Social skills, or the ability to know how to respond socially, can be learned.

- Teaching a child to say please and thank you is one thing, but teaching them how to know when to use this sentiment is another. Knowing when, where, how, and all the in-between rules of social expectation is the focal point of a social skills programme.

SOCIAL SKILLS SESSIONS (TAKEN FROM ASPERGER'S SUPPORT GROUP NETWORK HANDOUT, VICTORIA, AUSTRALIA 1997)

2–3 sessions per week

1. Small group – child and three class peers (good role models)

2. Select target behaviour:

    ◦ How to express anger
    ◦ How to express happiness
    ◦ How to express disappointment
    ◦ Hitting others: What are the better ways to communicate?
    ◦ Pushing roughly…how to be gentle
    ◦ Throwing sticks and other objects
    ◦ Throwing equipment
    ◦ Swearing
    ◦ Running off with another's property
    ◦ How to stop others taking what is yours
    ◦ Manners
    ◦ Listening skills
    ◦ Personal space
    ◦ Turn taking

3. Prioritise list and choose one

4. Small group session – students to act out the actual situation

5. Discuss:

    ◦ What happened?
    ◦ Why do you think it happened?
    ◦ How did you feel when it happened?
    ◦ What else could have been (i) said or (ii) done?

6. Practise, rehearse and role play the appropriate responses that have been suggested

7. Use real equipment

8. Use video camera to reinforce the auditory and visual message

9. Develop a script of 'say and do' strategies to learn and practise (perhaps keep in a small book or on a card to go into individual's pocket). These are safety phrases that need to be constantly reinforced. Sample phrases such as:

    'I need help'

    'I'm sorry'

    'I don't understand'

    'I'll try'

    'If I start feeling hot in the head I will count to ten under my breath'

10. Whatever skills are focused on there must be opportunities for practice in class and playground

11. Should the child make any attempt to use a skill it should be praised

12. Some type of reward system would intensify motivation to try

13. After play ask the child how things went and get the child's and others' perceptions of what happened.

Circle of friends – Peer support

∘ Meet regularly every week and follow up on the skills session

∘ Discuss the safety phrases – get input from all in the circle. When they would use them. How to use them – stand still, face the person, look at them and say I'm sorry

∘ Use the students to get ideas for the child to use

- Ask them to think of some ways they could use to help the child if they see something is happening

- Introduce some potential problem situations that you know will come up for the child

- Ask the circle to come up with solutions of how they may solve them. For example: What would you do if you lost your canteen money?

ASD and its impact upon self-esteem

Consider the following:

> 'Hop up on the couch for a minute while I talk to mum,' says the doctor. After hopping up and down on the couch for exactly one minute, I tell the doctor that his minute is up!

If you are an individual who takes words literally you might think that you are carrying out the doctor's instructions correctly. However, neuro-typical individuals might have interpreted the doctor's words quite differently. For example: They will sit down in the waiting room, or on a couch in the doctor's room and wait for Mum to finish speaking with the doctor. Imagine what it might mean to go through life, frequently misunderstanding neuro-typical implications!

When I am thinking or working on a task, if someone projects into my thinking or conversation I can feel almost violated! 'How dare they interrupt my space and distract me from my course. Didn't they understand that now I would have to start over again, recapture my thoughts or plans and schedule it all again!' Well actually, Wendy...No, they did not. You see...people talk to each other quite often. They don't need to put their thoughts on hold to do this, or even take time to go back to the beginning of their sequence of events after the conversation finishes. They can move from one thing to the other...most of the time.

What is my name?

You call my name. 'Come play a game'
'We want you here with us'
I hear you not, in Time forgot,
'Leave Wendy out. She's lost the plot'

You laugh at me, you run away,
I'm so glad you didn't stay.
But angry or discomfort now,
Could mean for me the biggest row!

To have a sense of 'good self-esteem' means to have a positive image of one's self, of one's identity. The word esteem itself means, 'to hold in high value…'. If a child grows and develops, over time, with the knowledge that they seem to upset people frequently, misunderstand the world around them often and constantly be in trouble for one thing or another…what is this going to do to their sense of being a valuable and positive contribution? I know that for me I felt a constant pull between being angry with others for failing to see my viewpoint, and despair at my inability to get things right.

'I want to be like Superman'
The answer to all things is 'He can',
His name gives hope,
He don't smoke dope.
He doesn't sit around and mope!

'Why can't I be like him?'
'Why do I not fit in?'
'I'm not the same, can't play your game,
What, I wonder, is in my name?'

Each of us has a script that is contributed to by both our own evaluation of self and the judgments made of us by others. What is written in your script? What is written in mine? Does it say positive things about you or about me? I believe that the internalised script that I live my life from can promote either a healthy sense of self or a very unhealthy one. If I feel valued and welcome, then the image I have of my worth and of myself should also be one of value.

> You called my name, your tone was soft.
> I looked at you with questioning eyes...
> 'It's OK' you said 'I will not scoff'.
> You noticed my fear and my surprise.
>
> 'Am I really welcome here?'
> 'You'll soon get fed up with me'.
> 'Well, if I do I'll just tell you so,
> We'll work it out, so have no fear'.
>
> 'But I so often get it wrong'.
> 'We all do that my friend'.
> 'But what if I hurt you?'
> 'You will, I'll mend'.
>
> So, how can I know if I should go,
> When to be fast, or to be slow?
> When to speak or silence show,
> It's your turn now, you have a go?
>
> We'll learn together, explore this land.
> Please allow me to hold your hand.
> It won't be easy, but we'll stand our ground,
> And come out triumphant, our friendship sound.
>
> (Lawson, 1999)

I know that I will never be neuro-typical. I will always have Asperger Syndrome. If I am to have a sense of pride and dignity, of high self-esteem, then I need to accept me as being who I am, value my sense of difference and work with my talents, attributes and disposition. I also need others to do the same!

As discussed earlier, being an individual with ASD means being unevenly skilled. This may mean an individual with ASD could expertly program a computer, but have huge problems with being disorganised, getting lost, using public transport, understanding others, and just the practical interactions of social situations. If their sense of value came from how good they were at everything –

achievement at school, work and home, being able to get into others' minds and be in tune with them all of the time – their self-esteem would be zilch. However, when self-esteem is high, rated on the fact that 'because I am, I am of value and any extras that I might possess are a bonus', then I can begin to build a positive picture of me!

Some practical tips

- ○ Focus in on the successes, not the failures, mistakes or 'could be improved'.

- ○ Discuss with your child/partner how they view their own achievements and/or progress.

- ○ If they think they are 'the best' ask them to explore their reasoning with you.

- ○ If they think they are 'the worst' ask them to explore their reasoning with you. Be careful not to use 'why' questions and always frame or structure your question so that they have a framework to respond in. Avoid open-ended questions, we don't know how to answer them!

- ○ Ask permission to work with them on any improvements they think might be necessary.

- ○ Ask permission to comment on their progress from your perspective.

- ○ Never assume that your comments for their improvement will be welcome. Either ask to be invited to comment or share your own experience with them, if allowed to, being careful NOT to compare yours to theirs. Just state the facts.

- ○ Always comment on any procedure that is done well, but aim not to comment when it is not!

- ○ Avoid using words that denote something is 'bad', 'rubbish', 'a mess', 'awful', 'could be better', 'poor', or 'incompetent'. Individuals with AS can be quick to pick up on all that they are not, rather than on what they are or could be!

- Offer lots and lots of positive reinforcement. I don't mean bribes, but well-timed approval is terrific. Not only does it let us know that we are OK, but it's useful in teaching us what the most appropriate response might be.

For example: 'Jenny I noticed that you banged the door much less when you were cross this morning and you used your mood clock to let me know how you were feeling instead.'

Help at school

Building self-esteem at home is terrific, but it needs to happen at school too. Knowing what a student's study skills are is a good place to begin to know what skills they will need most help with. Designing a student inventory for both study skills and social interaction is a must at the start of every new term. For example:
Study skills

- My hand writing is messy.

- I write too slowly.

- I don't like making decisions about what is (or is not) important when reading a book or journal article.

- I get distracted easily.

- I find it much easier when people use concrete examples; I don't know what to focus on in exams (and I always run out of time).

- I don't like sitting exams in strange places.

- I am a perfectionist.

- I'm not very good at problem solving (I don't like making decisions about particular responses).

- I find it hard to be motivated about some topics (and some topics upset me).

- I'm not always able to sit still for long periods.

- I'm not good at setting long-term goals.

- I am not good at getting to class on time or remembering all the equipment I need.

Social interaction

- I like to be left alone at times.
- I'm never sure when it's OK to interrupt in a conversation.
- I have difficulty knowing when people are joking.
- I find it quite hard to look people in the eye.
- I'm not very good at interpreting non-verbal cues.
- I'm not competitive (winning or losing is not important to me).
- I'm not good at conversing with others.
- I don't understand what is funny in many jokes.
- Others have said my speech is odd or eccentric.
- I find it difficult to make friends.
- I'm not very good with sarcasm or metaphor; I like people to say what they mean.
- I can get impatient when people don't understand me.

(Al-Mahmood *et al.* 1997, p.7)

The one thing the above inventory doesn't check or allow for are some of the skills that a student might be good at. Including these in a table would also be encouraging!

Some common difficulties
(By kind permission of Susan Moreno, July 2000, USA)
People with autism have trouble with organisational skills, regardless of their intelligence or age. Even a 'straight A' student with autism who has a photographic memory can be incapable of remembering to bring a pencil to class or of remembering a deadline for an assignment. In such cases, aid should be provided in the least restrictive way possible. Strategies could include having students put a picture of a

pencil on the cover of their notebooks or maintaining a list of assignments to be completed at home. Always praise the students when they remember something previously forgotten. Never denigrate or 'harp' at them when they fail. A lecture on the subject will not only NOT help, it will often make the problem worse. They may begin to believe they cannot remember to do or bring these things.

These students seem to have either the neatest or the messiest desks or lockers in the school. The one with the messiest desk will need your help in frequent cleanups of the desk or locker so that they can find things. Simply remember that they are probably not making a conscious choice to be messy. They are most likely incapable of this organisational task without specific training. Attempt to train them in organisational skills using small, specific steps.

People with autism have problems with abstract and conceptual thinking. Some may eventually acquire abstract skills, but others never will. When abstract concepts must be used, use visual cues, such as drawings or written words, to augment the abstract idea. Avoid asking vague questions such as 'Why did you do that?' Instead, say 'I did not like it when you slammed your book down when I said it was time for gym. Next time put the book down gently and tell me you are angry. Were you showing me that you did not want to go to gym, or that you did not want to stop reading?' Avoid asking essay-type questions. Be as concrete as possible in all your interactions with these students.

An increase in unusual or difficult behaviours probably indicates an increase in stress. Sometimes stress is caused by feeling a loss of control. Many times the stress will be alleviated only when the student physically removes himself from the stressful event or situation. If this occurs, a programme should be set up to assist the student in re-entering and staying in the stressful situation. When this occurs, a 'safe-place' or 'safe-person' may come in handy.

Do not take misbehaviour personally. The high-functioning person with autism is not a manipulative, scheming person who is trying to make life difficult. They are seldom, if ever, capable of being manipulative. Usually misbehaviour is the result of efforts to survive experiences which may be confusing, disorienting or frightening.

People with autism are, by virtue of their disability, egocentric. Most have extreme difficulty reading the reactions of others.

Most use and interpret speech literally. Until you know the capabilities of the individual, you should avoid:

- idioms (e.g. save your breath, jump the gun, second thoughts)

- double meanings (most jokes have double meanings)

- sarcasm (e.g. saying, 'Great!' after he has just spilled a bottle of ketchup on the table)

- nicknames

- 'cute' names (e.g. Pal, Buddy, Wise Guy).

Remember that facial expressions and other social cues may not work. Most individuals with autism have difficulty reading facial expressions and interpreting 'body language'.

If the student does not seem to be learning a task, break it down into smaller steps or present the task in several ways (e.g. visually, verbally, physically).

Avoid verbal overload. Be clear. Use shorter sentences if you perceive that the student is not fully understanding you. Although she or he probably has no hearing problem and may be paying attention, there may be a difficulty understanding your main point and identifying important information.

Prepare students for all environmental changes and changes in routine, such as assembly, substitute teacher and rescheduling. Use a written or visual schedule to prepare them for change.

Behaviour management can work, but if incorrectly used, it can encourage robot-like behaviour, provide only a short-term behaviour change or result in some form of aggression. Use positive and chronological age-appropriate behavioural procedures.

Consistent treatment and expectations from everyone is vital.

Be aware that normal levels of auditory and visual input can be perceived by the student as too much or too little. For example, the hum of fluorescent lighting is extremely distracting for some people with autism. Consider environmental changes such as removing 'visual clutter' from the room or seating changes if the student seems distracted or upset by his classroom environment.

If your high-functioning student with autism uses repetitive verbal arguments or repetitive verbal questions, you need to interrupt what can become a continuing, repetitive litany. Continually responding in a logical manner or arguing back seldom stops this behaviour. The subject of the argument or question is not always the subject which has upset them. More often the individual is communicating a feeling of loss of control or uncertainty about someone or something in the environment. Try requesting that they write down the question or argumentative statement. Then write down your reply. This usually begins to calm them down and stops the repetitive activity. If that doesn't work, write down the repetitive question or argument and ask them to write down a logical reply (perhaps one they think you would make). This distracts from the escalating verbal aspect of the situation and may give them a more socially acceptable way of expressing frustration or anxiety. Another alternative is role-playing the repetitive argument or question with you taking the student's part and having them answer you as they think you might.

Since these individuals experience various communication difficulties, do not rely on students with autism to relay important messages to their parents about school events, assignments, school rules, etc., unless you try it on an experimental basis with follow-up or unless you are already certain that the student has mastered this skill. Even sending home a note for their parents may not work. The student may not remember to deliver the note or may lose it before reaching home. Phone calls to parents work best until the skill can be developed. Frequent and accurate communication between the teacher and parent (or primary care-giver) is very important.

If your class involves pairing off or choosing partners, either draw numbers or use some other arbitrary means of pairing. Or ask an especially kind student if he or she would agree to choose the individual with autism as a partner before the pairing takes place. The student with autism is most often the individual left with no partner. This is unfortunate since these students could benefit most from having a partner.

Assume nothing when assessing skills. For example, the individual with autism may be a 'math whiz' in algebra, but not able to make simple change at a cash register. Or they may have an incredible memory about books they have read, speeches they have heard or sports statistics, but still may not be able to remember to bring a pencil to class. Uneven skills development is a hallmark of autism.

ASD, communication and computers

When one considers the information given above, and in the previous chapters, it is not difficult to appreciate the issues many individuals encounter with both the spoken and handwritten word. Teachers may complain that a child with ASD isn't tidy or careful enough in their handwriting and their assignment work. School projects can be very difficult for children who have spatial and organisational problems. However, work carried out on a computer can enable the child to present very differently.

Some teachers will still insist that the child practise their handwriting and will see offering the use of the computer as an excuse to avoid trying harder! This is comparable to withholding the use of sign language from children who are deaf and only allowing them to lip-read. Surely it is best to offer the children with ASD all the help that we can.

WHY COMPUTERS?

Computers do not present with social demands. They don't require you to smile at them or to listen to their opinion. They do not offer distracting stimuli to invade your concentration and interrupt your thinking! A computer will do exactly what you want it to do providing you inform it correctly of your request. Cutting out the middleman (don't take that literally) or decreasing the risk of sensory overload is very useful for individuals with ASD.

As an aid to education, leisure activities and communication with others, the computer is an asset that should not be overlooked. Being given the opportunity to use a computer as a tool for everyday life, both at home and at school, can mean the difference between feeling able to succeed and failure. A person will only try to achieve something so many times. If failure becomes the rule rather than the exception, then they will give up trying and resign themselves to alternatives. In adolescence and early adulthood the risk of developing mental illnesses (e.g. depression, social phobia and paranoia) are very high for individuals with ASD. Giving us appropriate forms of communication and a medium to express ourselves through, can aid healthy development and instil confidence along the rocky outcrops of life's stormy road.

According to Murray (2000), 'if you consult almost any text on what suits individuals on the autistic spectrum, you will find advice which can be applied with exceptional ease at a computer' (p.3). The following are features both of computers and of autism-friendly environments:

- reduced stimuli

- visual cues

- repetition

- clear cut rules

- lack of affect

- structure

- predictability

- controllability

- interest

- unhurried pace.

Oh how good it is to know that something is predictable! When all around me I am surrounded by a sea of uncertainty, when outcomes and consequences are too difficult to calculate, then my trusty computer comes to my rescue!

This People

Smiling, passing, moving to and fro,
This people.
Nodding, waving, crying, 'here we go'
This people.
Knowing, saying, accepting 'even though',
This people.
Belonging, staying, working, 'even so',
This people.
Freedom to be, freedom you see,
Is having the space to be truly me.
This people.

Check point

When relating to people who have an autism spectrum disorder it is important to remember the keys to understanding ASD these are:

- We are singly channelled (we either look or we listen, rather than doing both at once).

- We take words literally: 'Can you make your bed James?' Neuro-typicals mean 'Tidy your bed James', but a person with ASD might understand 'Do you know how a bed is made?' to which the answer might be 'Yes' or 'No'. But it might also mean that James does not comply with the request, because he hasn't understood the instruction as it was intended.

- We are not good at predicting consequences. For example: child picks up stone to throw it and is very upset when it lands upon another's head!

- We do not like change, because of difficulties with predicting outcomes.

Therefore it is good to:

- check out the autistic person's perception of what is being asked, demonstrated or said

○ teach that behaviours, emotions and desires can have particular facial and bodily expressions; explain what these are

○ rote learn rules for specific situations (e.g. we hug family members, not strangers; but, even when a person introduces themselves to you, we still class them as 'a stranger')

○ give time, whenever possible, to acclimatise to change and don't suddenly 'spring things' on to the person

○ use music, space, reassurance, relaxation and breathing exercises, a calm voice, and any other acceptable known anti-stressor, when the individual is anxious

○ place expectations into context via 'social stories'; this gives the individual a fuller picture of the 'whats', 'wherefores', 'whys', 'hows', and so on.

Key concepts

• A self-concept grows from the benefits of experience, as a result of personality attributes and as a result of 'upbringing'. To have a positive 'self-esteem' one must experience one's 'self' in a positive manner. This is difficult when we are being constantly told that we are disordered and impaired!

• 'How can I tell him he is different?' Let's turn it around and say something like: 'I have noticed that I do...whilst you do...' This is because we do things differently. We are different from one another.' When 'difference' is explored this way it does so with equality and respect. It does not attack self-esteem or place an individual into a place where their 'difference' is experienced negatively and with regret.

• We need to recognise and accommodate 'difference'.

Point to ponder

Treat others as you would like them to treat you.

CHAPTER 10

Social Stories and Language

The role of social story telling – as a helping strategy (see Gray 2000)

Social stories are a great way to explain everyday events that an individual with ASD may encounter. Unlike telling a child a bedtime story, social stories are based in reality and can best be told when a child is attentive and happy. This may be when a child is wanting their questions answered or it may be whilst they are jumping on a trampoline, swinging on a swing, splashing in the pool, and any other time when they are content. Social stories need to take into account *intent, context* and *scale.*

> *Example:* A parent explains to their six-year-old child with ASD that they will have visitors whom the child hasn't seen before. The visitors are coming to talk to the parent. The child will play with the children, whom the child knows well, in the neighbour's house, next door. When the visitors have left, the parent will come over to the neighbour's house to fetch the child. Visual aids to the story are very useful. Sometimes cut-outs from magazines can be used, sometimes real photos.

When telling a 'social story' it is very important to choose one's words carefully. Avoiding the use of words that can be mistakenly taken literally is useful. However, if this cannot be achieved, then checking on the child's understanding is vital.

> *Example of a non-social story:* Teacher says to Johnny 'Johnny, this is your peg. You can hang your hat, coat and school bag upon this peg. When you need to get something from your bag, you

can come to find it here. You can take what you want (e.g. lunch box) from your bag and place it back upon your hook. At the time when you get ready to leave school to go home, you can come to your peg, take your hat, coat and bag off the peg, and prepare for going home.'

The above story might be understood by neuro-typicals quite well, but Johnny might think that the peg is his and he may try to take it off the wall to keep for himself! In order to explain the situation to Johnny so that he understands it would be wise to say 'Johnny, this is *the* peg' and not 'this is *your* peg'!

Coping strategies and language

In every situation there is a coping strategy. How do we find it?

- PRIORITISE
- COLLABORATE
- COMMUNICATE

Prioritise

- Choose which issues demand immediate attention (e.g. injury to self or others).
- Deal with one issue at a time.
- Stick to it (for a decent period of time, before exploring next issue).

Collaborate

- Ask questions, identify stresses, and key issues (e.g. 'Turn lights off...Is that better?').
- Eliminate possible stressors for overload (e.g. lights, music, conversation, noise, activity).
- Establish a 'stress-free zone'.

Communicate

Things to avoid	**Things to do/include**
Stating outcomes (e.g. we eat lunch at twelve o'clock)	Estimate outcomes (e.g. we usually eat...)
We always...	Sometimes
Using metaphors	Speak plainly
Using complex words	Speak simply
Talking without respect	Take time to value
Not checking what's been understood	Check understanding
Failure to listen	Really listen
Being in a rush	Do not be in a hurry
Failure to give advance warning of change	Prepare for change

Some useful considerations for stress reduction

- Communication...   *Am I being clear and concise?*

- Collaboration...   *What has been understood?*

- Cooperation...   *What factors might hinder cooperation?*

- Teamwork...   *Create communication between family, school, work place.*

- Reassurance...   *Is security and a sense of well-being being fostered?*

Relevant key issues that impact upon ASD individuals:

- Anxiety

- Fear

- Frustration

- Anger

Single interests

Single interests, or particular interests, are another of our varied skills! I have the ability to stay focused for hours! However, this ability only applies to areas of my interest. Not that many years ago I would always begin a conversation with 'Did you know...?' Or, I might have said 'And what do you know about...?' It never occurred to me to begin a conversation with such niceties as 'Hello' or 'Hi, how are you?' I really wasn't interested in others talking so much as I was in having them listen to what I needed to say! Over time I learnt that if I wanted to engage in ongoing conversation, then I had to let other people tell me their stories as well.

Overload

As I have stated before, individuals with ASD get 'overloaded' very easily. Most information being given to a person enters their consciousness via the senses (sight, sound, touch, and so on). For myself and many other ASD individuals all the sensory information that comes from people in any situation (such as conversational noise, movement of people, clothing, doors, lights, and so on) soon becomes an overwhelming concoction.

Learning to recognise overload is very important. Prevention is better than cure! Each individual is different and, therefore, will have different strengths, weaknesses and limitations. Ultimately it is in the individual's best interest to learn to recognise these themselves. In the meantime though it is up to the parent, teacher or carer to aid the understanding of this process.

Concentration

Concentration span for many of us as ASD individuals is very limited and we soon tire. Using subject material that we are interested in is very helpful and will facilitate longer interest. At school it was always difficult for me to learn about things that I was not interested in. I just couldn't see the point. Temple Grandin (1996) talks about 'thinking in pictures' and I certainly am one of those people who do this. I have wondered if this might have some bearing on the matter. Maybe I lacked the connections to build appropriate pictures if the material to be learned didn't have a familiar component to it. Maybe, if I didn't have a picture for it I couldn't think it?

Simple tasks?

The following is adapted from an article I published in *Autism* (Lawson 1998c). From January to June in 1997 I studied at a university in the UK. I was living in halls, and as a consequence these are some of the difficulties that I encountered.

Dining rooms, TV rooms, the games room and the bar are all terrifying places and I will avoid them if possible. Unfortunately I had initially paid full board so my meals were included in my accommodation. Lining up for meals was very uncomfortable. If students had stood in an orderly line, single file, it might have been workable. However, they tended to push in, move across to be with other students that they appeared to know, and stand three or four abreast. I did not know what they might do next! When I finally arrived at the meal counter I took whatever was given to me, located a table with an empty seat to sit down at and attempted to eat my meal. Again, unfortunately, I needed more time to think about what I wanted to eat, so because I hadn't taken the time I often ended up with a meal I didn't like or couldn't eat!

I did try arriving early, but the queue just built up around me. Then I tried organising a meal with the kitchen, arriving late and just collecting it before they closed. However, I then had no choice over what was kept for me. In the end I moved into self-catering halls and this solved the problem. From then on, during the remainder of my stay I lived on baked beans, fruit and cereal!

The other example I'll give you is the laundry. I was supposed to change one sheet from my bed every week. I didn't know how to do this (should I carry the sheet in a plastic bag, tuck it under my arm or what?). I didn't change any sheets for five weeks. Then I saw another student taking a sheet to the laundry, so I did as they were doing. The laundry lady said 'Top to bottom dear'. I hadn't any idea what she was talking about so, as usual, I just smiled.

It was several weeks later, after I had been taking my one sheet to the laundry, that I realised what she had meant. I helped my friend change the sheet on her bed. As we did so she said 'top to bottom' and placed the top sheet on the mattress, using the clean sheet as the top sheet under her quilt. 'Oh,' I said, 'is that what you are supposed to do?' I had simply been taking my top sheet off the bed and putting the clean one on in its place. I hadn't changed the bottom sheet at all!

I must stress again, that this perspective is both from my own personal experience and from my studies. ASD individuals have different personalities and, therefore, their autistic expression will vary accordingly. Some individuals are 'in your face', up front, perhaps extroverts, others are shy, withdrawn, perhaps introverts, and so on. It really is important to see us as individuals.

As I have said, most ASD people find their sense of security in their rules, rituals and continuity of roles. Therefore, it is very distressing when life does not go according to our expectations. This is one reason why we manipulate our environment and the individuals that share it with us. However, when we feel safe and reassured, our need to manipulate decreases.

Sharpley *et al.* (1997) found that families who were supported and who experienced 'hope' for the future, suffered less anxiety than those who were 'out there alone'. Understanding ASD, being part of a support group, having autism friendly teachers and other professionals, are some of the key factors in promoting a sense of hope and vision for the future.

Today, I 'connect' more readily with life and enjoy both family and friends around me. I am happy 'alone', especially when I can pursue my own interests, and I have developed strategies that enable me more than just to cope with life's demands. However, for more than 40 years I lived with intense feelings of confusion, frustration, depression and isolation. This does not have to be the sentence for our children and autistic adults today. With appropriate support and intervention their lives, and those of their families, can be quite different!

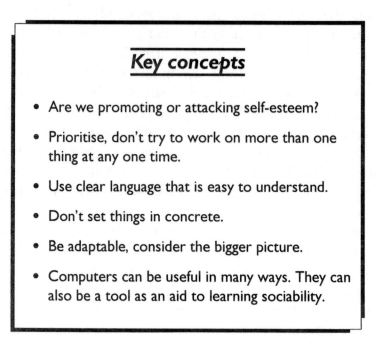

Key concepts

- Are we promoting or attacking self-esteem?

- Prioritise, don't try to work on more than one thing at any one time.

- Use clear language that is easy to understand.

- Don't set things in concrete.

- Be adaptable, consider the bigger picture.

- Computers can be useful in many ways. They can also be a tool as an aid to learning sociability.

Point to ponder

Words like *usually* and *sometimes* take away black/white expectations. This is very useful. It can be supportive in preventing the forming of absolutes! For example: 'We usually have juice with our breakfast' is a better option than 'We always have juice with our breakfast'.

Epilogue

Since learning to read at the age of nine and then, at the age of 13, connecting to the idea that books were an echo of spoken language, I have come to love words and writing. *Life As an Alien*, my first self-published book of poetry, was an exploration of life as a person whom others encountered as being 'different' to them. I love the way words can portray meaning in such a concise and thrifty way. In poetry, even though one has been economical with one's expression, the sentiment is encountered and lingers to open doors to a shared experience.

Writing my second book *Life Behind Glass*, an autobiographical account of growing up with undiagnosed Asperger Syndrome (AS), helped to consolidate and draw together so many of my life experiences. After gaining a diagnosis of AS at the age of 42, I was finally able to put away my misdiagnosis of schizophrenia and intellectual disability. My life has continued to bless, encourage and frustrate me.

As a young woman my roots were very much based in the roles and expectations of a 'working-class' family. I lived my life seemingly without resources and without support. I felt that my future seemed grey and very limited. Upon coming to Australia, gaining a university education and accessing ongoing friendships, my future now appears brighter and I have hope. This hope is not only for myself, but for my family and for those others who will also be diagnosed with an autism spectrum delay.

My life journey to date has taken me through previously uncharted waters. I have married and divorced. I birthed four children. My third youngest, Mattie, whilst in his prime and only nineteen years of age, was killed by a very drunk driver. In fact both men were killed, quite needlessly. Although Matt will always live on in our hearts, we have all been cheated of knowing the future that could have been.

After living in our family home for 13 years (the longest I had ever lived anywhere) in August 1999 we decided to leave the city suburbs and have a 'sea change'. I had always wanted to live by the ocean. The move meant leaving the children (by then all grown up) who wanted to stay close to their friends and careers, and venture out into unknown waters. I love our new home. To date we have been here just 15 months. I am able to walk along sandy beaches, bask in the joy of seeing so many of the coastal birds that grace the shores near my home, and listen to the roar of the great southern ocean. I have found my paradise.

When I was younger so much of what I now enjoy seemed out of reach. I still find it hard to interact with others, but I have grown in confidence and take more risks with being myself. If being who I am is upsetting to others, I can now view this as being their issue, not mine. I am determined to reach the outer limits of awareness, soar through intimidation and fly upon the wings of knowledge. This can happen even in the face of ignorance, bigotry and oppression. Indeed it must!

My life has moved on from one lived in isolation, conformity and performance. I now anticipate good things. I expect the best and encounter life in every manner of the word. I once read: 'Without a vision the people perish.' I hope that this book will inspire vision and, in doing so, will enable many others to experience 'life' and live it to the max!

Clothing The Shadows

Though often torn and tormented my outer self struggled on.
There were times the inner 'Wendy' felt completely dead and
    gone.
In order to resurrect her, 'Love' called and begged her 'come'.
Wendy answered that sweet call and now true 'life' has begun.
The journey leading from darkness to dawn has taken me by
    the hand.

Oft full of fear and unsure of the way, my feet have at last
found firm ground.
Although a solitary traveller, I've shared with many a
'Highway'.
To mark the company of another gives light and can brighten
the day.

The empty shadows so naked and plain that haunted my every
step,
Have retreated from their hiding place, their doubts have all
been swept.
When I am tempted to look their way I turn instead to hear
another say,
'Wendy, walk with me today, leave the shadows, Let's away'.

I need the prompt of another's hand when I forget how to take
my stand.
I value words of truth and light that help me find the way to
fight.
I no longer walk in the shadows. I no longer feel estranged.
I've found my place, a true delight, a forest, ocean or mountain
range.

For, wherever my feet wonder now, I can sure-footed be.
I no longer fear the shadows, but welcome the chance to be
free.
I can understand how shadows form and why they dance at
night.
They need the light to help them show but once in clothes,
they must go!

So, clothing the shadows is now my heart felt song.
I long that others will also join this throng.
Don't let those empty shadows dictate to who you are.
Instead, you lift your head up high,
Laugh loud at them, kiss them goodbye.
Goodbye, goodbye, goodbye.

APPENDIX 1
Questions I Have Been Asked

When did you first realise you were different?
I think that I always knew that I was not like others…but I didn't know why or how.

How did it affect your family relationships? For example did your parents realise you were different? In retrospect, could they have done anything more to help you as a child?
My parents were so busy with having a large family and often running their own business that Wendy's idiosyncrasies were just 'Wendy being Wendy'! I was mostly left to my own devices. At times I felt as if there was much anger directed towards me, but I never understood why. I didn't really receive the help and support that I could have benefited from, as a child.

As a child, did you find it hard to make friends with other children, or were you not really interested in that?
This was very difficult and I had very little success! I was viewed as 'a know-all' and the only way that I could relate to other children was if we had an interest in common (e.g. dogs or medicine – in my teens I read medical books because they fascinated me). I was interested, at a distance, in having a friend…but I lacked the social 'know-how' of reci-procity and, quite often would go overboard to 'buy' friends, influence others with knowledge, or become their 'helper' to earn a friend.

Did you have rituals and obsessions at an early age? If so how did they develop? And what benefit did you derive from them? Did new rituals and obsessions replace old ones? Do you (or did you) feel that you needed to control them?
Yes, I always had rituals and obsessions!!! Yes, they changed over time. However, they were always based around my interests: animals, insects,

medicine… I like to wear clothes that are familiar (new ones hang around for ages) eat foods that are the same (I could live on baked beans on toast; mashed potato, carrots and gravy; or McDonald's!!). I hated it when routines changed and would become quite miserable, almost lose motivation for anything. I needed to be sure of what would happen; I need to know so that I can know what will happen, what to expect… I am still like this today; however, I am more adaptable now than I was as a child!

What was your experience of school like? Did you have the same problems at school as you did at college in the UK?

YUK!!!! at first I was interested in school but after getting into trouble constantly and not understanding what was going on around me, school became a nightmare. I was bullied and teased mercilessly. I just wanted the world to stop so that I could get off and go back to being with my dog!! This did change when I left school and moved on to college, however. I think it changed because I am academic, more than social, and at college and uni I met others who were more like me…interested in study.

What about sensitivities to sound, touch, light, etc. – are these a problem? If so, can you explain how and why this is, and whether they have improved as you have got older?

Yes, my ears are very sensitive to particular sounds and certain noises really hurt me…even today. I wear tinted glasses to help me cope with the light that hurts my eyes, and I only wear cotton next to my skin because of discomfort with how other materials feel. I don't know why this is so, but it always has been and I haven't noticed much improvement over time.

Are you able to empathise and understand other people's emotions? Can you tell someone's state of mind by looking at their face?

I'm not good at 'reading' another's body language…I often 'feel' that if someone is unhappy then it must be my fault. I make others angry…I am learning that this isn't always the case but I still find this difficult. I don't 'feel' the emotions of others, unless it impacts upon myself. However, I have learnt how to 'listen' to others and how to ask them how they are feeling and what this might mean for them. I am naturally inquisitive about human behaviour and driven to understand both myself and others. This means asking lots and lots of questions all of the time which can be very demanding on people and is not always appreciated!

What are your views on the various therapies/treatments currently available such as AIT, Lovaas, Options, Irlen lenses, and so on? Do you have a view on these? Do you think any of these would have been of benefit to you as a child?

Some therapies are very good for some, and different therapies work for different people. The things to look out for are: the length of time and effectiveness that the particular therapy has a history of; the cost to implement and how intrusive it is upon the whole family; is it documented and supported by known authorities and does your child seem to benefit from it? The one thing that all agree on is that early intervention and keeping a child connected to life are the very best things that you can do for any child with autism.

How did you learn to compensate for being different? Did you have to learn social skills by trial and error? If so, how? And do you find that these social skills become easier with practice?

Yes, I did learn social skills by trial and error!! Yes, they have become easier over time (much, much time). I compensate, if you like, by specialising in one area and becoming good at that. Then I have something to offer; something that others are interested in.

What situations do you find the most difficult to deal with? Do you find it difficult talking to strangers who try to start up a conversation with you? Are you happy to talk about the difficulties that Asperger Syndrome gives you?

Anything that I am not in control of! Public transport; pubs, clubs, parties, and so on. I love to talk about things I am interested in and will generally steer a conversation that way. I am very happy to talk about anything to do with autism/Asperger's…even, or especially, if it is to do with my own experience.

What's the most important advice you would give to a parent whose
child has just been diagnosed with Asperger Syndrome?
This is difficult…there are several things that a parent would benefit
from, for example remembering that their child will grow up and they
won't stay the way they are today! Pervasive developmental DELAY is
just that, DELAY not CANCELLATION! A parent will need to look
after themselves and take time to do this (e.g. foster time out for relaxation and pleasure; attend to personal relationships with partner and
any other family members…other children). A parent needs lots of
support and they need to know that that's OK. Teachers, psychologists
and other professionals will not always see things the same way that a
parent does. This can be upsetting, but, as parents we need to fight for
our children and not be put off by the ignorance of others. All of this
means that for parents it is better to join with others and share the experience, rather than try to go it alone!

Commonly Asked Questions About Autism

Parts of what follow first appeared in *The Newsletter* of the Autism Association Of Western Australia, Vol. 2, April 2000.

What caused my child to be autistic?
Currently we do not know the full cause of autism. We do know that, in layman's terms, messages in the brain can seem confusing for the autistic person; therefore, their responses and reactions can seem egocentric, bizarre, detached and non-communicative.

Researchers say that autism probably has a genetic base. There is nothing that a parent can do to stop their child from being autistic. Autism is a lifelong condition.

Can my child's autism be controlled?
Autism in itself does not respond to medication or other conservative treatments. However, some researchers claim that music therapy, exercise therapy, behavioural intervention therapy, vitamin and diet regimes do have an influence upon autism and that programmes organised by trained persons can enhance or maximise potential for the individual with autism.

If the individual with autism has some condition that needs medical treatment (e.g. epilepsy, diabetes, depression, etc.) then medical advice should be followed.

Will my child be able to go to a normal school?
It is good to be guided by trained staff who know you and your child. The most important thing is that the educational programme developed for the child meets his or her needs and includes appropriate teaching based on an understanding of the learning profile of the child with autism. Some children are best taught in an autism specialist class or school, where the environment is highly structured. However, many

children with autism can be included in regular classes. Whatever the setting, the school needs to understand exactly the child's strengths and difficulties and the manner in which the child with autism most easily learns.

Will my child become less autistic as he or she grows older?

Most people with autism, especially if they are not intellectually disabled, want very much to achieve their goals. Therefore, over time they will develop strategies to help them learn and understand the world around them.

This means that they themselves can usually control their autistic behaviours. At times of stress, however, they may revert to autistic behaviour as an automatic response. So, yes, able adults with autism are not usually plagued by the same fears and anxieties as they were when they were children.

What is the incidence of autism?

Currently, considering the wider spectrum of ASD, the research puts this at approximately 5 in 1000 births.

What is the gender ratio?

At one time ASD was considered to be a predominantly 'male' disability. Now it appears to be almost as common in girls as it is in boys.

What are the main criteria used for diagnosis?

1. Difficulty with social relationships
2. Difficulty with verbal and non-verbal communication, and with imaginative play.
3. Markedly restricted activities and interests (often engages in obsessive behaviour).
4. Onset during the child's first three years.

What is the generally accepted cause of autism?

Autism is a neurobiological difference. The causes are still being researched.

What is the range of intellectual abilities?

Intellectual ability ranges from severe intellectual disability to normal and above normal intelligence.

What is the best approach for developing language skills?

Programmes need to be based on individual strengths and needs. A substantial body of evidence supports people with autism being visual learners. A visual system to suit the child of either symbols, pictures, the printed word or any combination of these should be used to support and augment communication development.

Can drug therapy be useful?

Medication has no primary role in autism, in a curative sense. However, carefully prescribed and monitored medication is occasionally necessary to stabilise behaviour or control epilepsy.

Are there some people with autism who do exceptionally well?

Some people with autism have exceptional skills in areas such as music, memory, mathematics and motor skills. Not all people with autism, however, have such skills.

How can problems with behaviour be managed?

The most effective behaviour management approach is one which provides people with skills to function in their everyday life and is non-aversive (i.e. one that does not use punishment). Behaviour problems can occur for a variety of reasons – a mismatch between the demands of an environment and the child's skill; frustration; pain; distress; the only means of communication. It is important, therefore, to consider these issues and act accordingly.

Is autism an emotional problem?

Autism is a neurobiological disorder. It is not caused by anything that parents do, or do not do, or by any other aspect of the child's home management.

Do people with autism marry and lead independent lives?
Some people with autism marry. Follow-ups of adults with autism, however, indicate that most will require support throughout their lives in varying degrees.

Do people with autism have physical disabilities?
Because autism can be associated with other conditions, some people with autism do have physical disabilities. However, most people with autism are very healthy and have a normal life expectancy.

What is Asperger Syndrome?
Researchers still do not agree on whether Asperger Syndrome is different from or the same as autism. It is seen to be part of the autism continuum, though, and is usually associated with average or better intellectual ability. People with Asperger Syndrome develop language, sometimes highly grammatical and pedantic, but may use it in unusual ways. They may also have problems with social relationships.

APPENDIX 3
Exercises

Below are some written exercises that will aid and support your learning. These exercises are also a useful tool to finding possible solutions to everyday problems that individuals with ASD and their families may encounter. The chapter heading above each set of exercises will indicate to you the area of reading you need to consult to help you with answering the questions found in each exercise.

Chapter 1

- Explain the cognitive processes informing ASD experience.
- How could one assist the development of 'theory of mind' in an individual with ASD?
- What do the words 'intent, context and scale' refer to?

Chapter 2

- Can it be useful to be given a 'label'?
- What are the differences between the various 'labels' along the ASD continuum?
- What types of circumstances and situations lead to overload?

Chapter 3

- How might personality influence ASD experience?
- Can IQ assessments be useful within the field of ASD?
- What might be some typical health concerns for individuals with ASD?

Chapter 4 and Chapter 8

- ○ What might be some common reasons for individuals with ASD forming obsessions?

- ○ How can self-injury be addressed?

- ○ What might help an ASD individual who is living with inappropriate obsessions and compulsions?

Chapter 5

- ○ How might neuro-typical individuals experience stress differently to the individual with ASD?

- ○ What might be some appropriate supports for parents of ASD individuals?

- ○ What might be some appropriate supports for individuals with ASD?

Chapter 6

- ○ What might be some of the issues families could face when seeking a diagnosis?

- ○ What are some typical behaviours of ASD individuals?

- ○ How can depression and other mental health issues be prevented or treated in individuals with ASD?

Chapter 7

- ○ Is it true that individuals with ASD lack feelings and emotions?

- ○ What might be happening for ASD individuals where emotions and feelings are concerned?

- ○ Do all ASD individuals display the same types of difficulties?

- How might the difficulties experienced by individuals with ASD manifest themselves at the various points on the ASD continuum?

Chapter 8

- What might be the message behind some seemingly challenging behaviours in ASD?

- How can anger and aggression be 'managed' within the world of ASD?

- How might rejection and failure be experienced by individuals with ASD? What can we do about it?

Chapter 9

- How can we support and encourage a healthy self-esteem?

- When should we explore the issues of 'being different' for ASD individuals?

- What kinds of 'things' could be helpful in an educational environment, such as school, for ASD individuals?

Chapter 10

- What are the essential components to building a 'social story'?

- Are social stories designed to change behaviour or inform social understanding?

- What kind of language should we use when communicating with individuals with ASD?

Criteria for Assessment of Autism

The following diagnostic criteria for autism are based on
The Diagnostic and Statistical Manual of Mental Disorders (DSM-IV).

*A1. Qualitative impairment in social interaction as manifested
by at least two of the following:*

- Marked impairment in the use of multiple non-verbal behaviours such as eye-to-eye gaze, facial expression, body postures and gestures to regulate social interaction.

- Failure to develop peer relationships appropriate to developmental level.

- Lack of spontaneous seeking to share enjoyment, interests or achievements with other people (e.g. by a lack of showing, bringing, or pointing at objects).

- Lack of social or emotional reciprocity.

*2. Qualitative impairments in communication as manifested by
at least one of the following:*

- Delay in, or total lack of, the development of spoken language (not accompanied by an attempt to compensate through alternative modes of communication such as gesture or mime).

- In individuals with adequate speech, marked impairment in the ability to initiate or sustain a conversation with others.

- Stereotyped and repetitive use of language or idiosyncratic language.

- Lack of varied, spontaneous make-believe play or social imitative play appropriate to developmental level.

3. Restricted repetitive and stereotyped patterns of behaviour, interests, and activities, as manifested by at least one of the following:

- ◦ Encompassing preoccupation with one or more stereotyped and restricted patterns of interest that is abnormal either in intensity or focus.

- ◦ Apparently inflexible adherence to specific, non-functional routines or rituals.

- ◦ Stereotyped and repetitive motor mannerisms (e.g. hand or finger flapping or twisting, or complex whole-body movements).

- ◦ Persistent preoccupations with parts of objects.

B. Delays or abnormal functioning in at least one of the following areas, with onset prior to age 3 years:

- ◦ social interaction

- ◦ language as used in social communication

- ◦ symbolic or imaginative play.

C. The disturbance is not better accounted for by Rett's disorder or childhood disintegrative disorder.

APPENDIX 5

Name **Wendy Bateman**   **Autumn** Term 196**3**

Year	**I**	Stream **B**	Term Grade	Exam. Position	No. in Form	Position

Subject	Grade	Comment
ENGLISH LANGUAGE	C-	Good ideas spoilt by carelessness. She must work much harder. All work in book must be done in ink.
ENGLISH LITERATURE	D+	She must work much harder.
RELIGIOUS KNOWLEDGE	C	Wendy's oral work is good. I don't see enough of her written work. *A.M.*
FRENCH		
HISTORY	C-	Oral work excellent. Written homework is invariably forgotten, not given in or badly done. If is time Wendy grew up a little. *J.*
GEOGRAPHY	D	Is rather untidy *J.*
MATHEMATICS	C	Wendy does her best, she finds this subject difficult. *P.A.N*
SCIENCE	D	Does not take enough care. Seems almost incapable of doing as she is told
DOMESTIC SCIENCE		
NEEDLEWORK	C-	Fairly good *M.S.*
ART	.C	Wendy's work is spoilt by carelessness and untidiness.
CRAFT	C	
MUSIC	C+	Usually Good. *A.M.*
PHYSICAL EDUCATION		Works well – Swimming shows promise. *E.W.*

GRADES:—A, excellent; B, ~~very~~ good; C, satisfactory; D, weak; E, poor.

ATTENDANCE and PUNCTUALITY: Quite good – Is late too often.

GENERAL REPORT: Wendy will have to realise that she has to work hard. She must get herself organised, so that she has the right things at the right time eg. a pen – Too much of her work is incorrect, done in the wrong place, or not done at all. She must WAKE UP.   J.W. Talbot.   FORM MISTRESS

PARENT'S SIGNATURE J. M. Bateman   T Laws :   HEAD MISTRESS

Rational-Emotive Therapy's ABC Theory of Emotional Disturbance

"Men (people) are disturbed not by things, but by the views which they take of them." (Epictetus, 1st Century AD)

It is not the event, but rather it is our interpretation of it, that causes our emotional reaction.

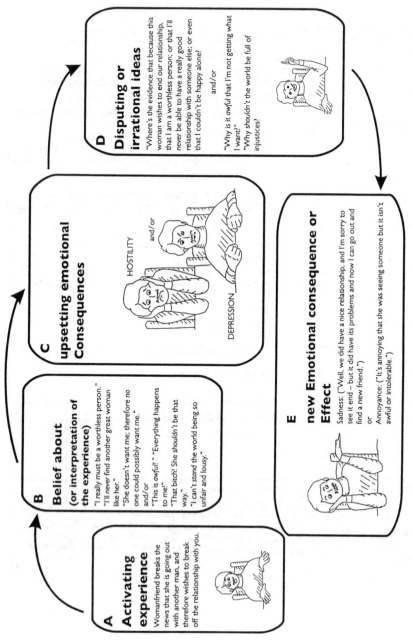

D Disputing or irrational ideas

"Where's the evidence that because this woman wishes to end our relationship, that I am a worthless person; or that I'll never be able to have a really good relationship with someone else; or even that I couldn't be happy alone?

and/or

"Why is it *awful* that I'm not getting what I want?"
"Why *shouldn't* the world be full of injustices?

C upsetting emotional Consequences

HOSTILITY   and/or

DEPRESSION

B Belief about (or interpretation of the experience)

"I really must be a worthless person." "I'll never find another great woman like her."

"She doesn't want me; therefore no one could possibly want me."
and/or
"This is *awful!* " "Everything happens to me!"
"That bitch! She *shouldn't* be that way."
"I can't *stand* the world being so unfair and lousy."

A Activating experience

Womanfriend breaks the news that she is going out with another man, and therefore wishes to break off the relationship with you.

E new Emotional consequence or Effect

Sadness: ("Well, we did have a nice relationship, and I'm sorry to see it end – but it did have its problems and now I can go out and find a new friend.")
or
Annoyance: ("It's annoying that she was seeing someone but it isn't awful or intolerable.")

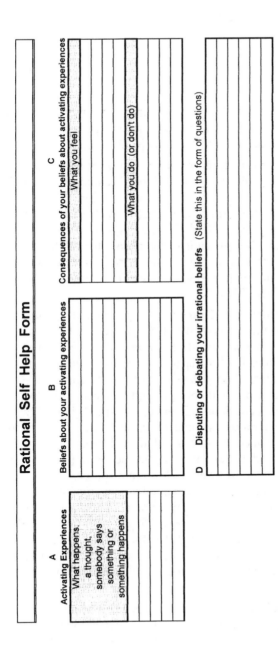

Rational Self Help Form

A
Activating Experiences
What happens.
a thought,
somebody says
something or
something happens

B
Beliefs about your activating experiences

C
Consequences of your beliefs about activating experiences
What you feel

What you do (or don't do)

D   Disputing or debating your irrational beliefs   (State this in the form of questions)

E   Effects of disputing or debating your irrational beliefs

Rational Beliefs (your wants/desires)

Emotional Effects (appropriate feelings)

Behavioral Effects (desirable behaviours)

Glossary

Anxiety is seen and felt as a result of inner conflict. It is the term given to describe the response of the human organism to perceived threat to one's welfare or safety (Clinebell 1991).

Asperger Syndrome (AS) is a form of autism originally described by Hans Asperger in 1944. Eisenmajer (1996), Rickarby *et al.* (1991) and Wing (1992) are among researchers who believe there is much evidence for an autism continuum, of which AS is seen to be closer to, or the same as, 'high-functioning autism'. AS, therefore, refers to a specific autistic diagnosis where a child's autistic spectrum disorder displays all the attributes of autism, but the child has normal language development and does not have an intellectual disability (DSM-IV).

Autism Spectrum Disorder (ASD) refers to a spectrum of autistic disorders described in the DSM-IV (1994) under the heading of 'Pervasive Developmental Disorders' (I prefer 'delays'). ASD is illustrated in individuals who display poor knowledge of social rules and social skills; show delayed, absent or stereotypical language; have little or no 'theory of mind'; display repetitive and/or compulsive behaviours and are egocentric (Wing 1992). ASD relates to a condition that impacts upon a person's ability to understand and interact with the world around them. It affects 5 children in 1000 and is found throughout the world (Prior 1998). 'Autism is one of the most severe childhood disorders characterized by qualitative and quantitative impairments in two way social interaction, communication and a marked restriction in range of interests and activities' (Boyd 1992, p.63). Although the idea of an autism continuum is popular (for example some researchers believe Kanner's autism (classic autism) and Asperger Syndrome are terms used to describe 'types' of ASD), this is still a topic for debate.

Central Coherence: A characteristic of usual (neuro-typical) information-processing appears to be the tendency to draw together diverse information to construct higher-level meaning in context (Happé 1998).

Cognition: Mental operations such as thinking, conceiving, reasoning, symbolising, insight, expectancy, complex rule use, imagery, belief, intention, problem solving, and so forth (Reber 1995).

Depression, for the purpose of this book, will be thought of as a term describing a state of sadness, helplessness and despair (Kennedy and Charles 1994).

Echolalia: The compulsive and apparently senseless repetition of a word or phrase just spoken by another person. Sometimes in autism, echolalia can be a repetition of phrases heard from television, radio or over a speaker. It can be a word or phrase invented by the individual and it can present as delayed echolalia, being repeated some time after it has been heard.

High Functioning Autism: Autism without intellectual disabilty.

Idiosyncratic Language refers to language used that is apparently born from ignorance, without knowledge, or from being in a totally private, inaccessible state.

Intellectual Disability is said to occur when an individual scores at or below 70 on an IQ test. Scoring can vary typically from below 50 up to 70, and the individual is said to be either severely, moderately or mildly intellectually disabled (DSM-IV).

Language: '...conventional symbols through which we convey meaning...the medium through which we code our feelings, thoughts, ideas and experiences...' (Reber 1995, p.406).

Neuro-typical, for the purpose of this book, will refer to non-autistic individuals who are of 'normal' intelligence and do not have either an intellectual, social or communication disability. The author recognises that this term could be ambiguous and notes that it is only used to separate people with an autism spectrum disorder from those people without such a disorder.

Obsessive-Compulsive Disorders are disorders 'whose symptoms are obsessions (persistent and irrational thoughts or wishes) and compulsions (uncontrollable, repetitive acts), which seem to be defences against anxiety' (Gleitman 1991, p.A42).

Pervasive Developmental Disorder (PDD) is the general term or heading located in the DSM-IV that ASD diagnosis come under. It implies that a person's development in the areas of social skill, communication, interests, activities and behaviour 'deviant relative to the individual's developmental level or age'. Not all children with PDD will gain a diagnosis of autism or Asperger Syndrome. Some are said to have a pervasive developmental disorder not otherwise specified (PDD-NOS).

Pronominal Reversal: A speech problem in which the individual refers to himself or herself as 'he', 'she' or 'you', and uses 'I' or 'me' in referring to others.

Socialisation is a 'process whereby an individual acquires the knowledge, values, facility with language, social skills and social sensitivity enabling them to integrate into and behave adaptively within a society' (Reber, 1995 p.732).

Social Stories: Putting the different things that are allowed to happen into the social context via a story (e.g. at recess we usually eat our morning snack before we go out to play) (Gray 2000).

Stereotypical Language: Language that appears pedantic, rigid, set or generally associated with a particular culture.

Theory of Mind or 'mind reading' refers to the ability to comprehend the fact that 'others' have their own thoughts, emotions and opinions, which may be different from one's own. Sometimes it is referred to as having the ability 'to put oneself into another's shoes' or 'to see things from another's perspective'.

Unsatisfactory Stress Levels are, according to Green and Shellenberger (1991), an emotional mental response to perceived threats and challenges from either external stimuli or internal stimuli, such as thoughts.

References

Al-Mahmood, R., Mclean, P., Powell, E. and Ryan, J. (1997) 'Towards success in tertiary study.' Commonwealth Dept. of Education, Employment, Training and Youth Affairs, University of Melbourne.

American Psychiatric Association (1994) *Diagnostic and Statistical Manual of Mental Disorders* (4th ed.) Washington, DC: American Psychiatric Association.

Asperger Syndrome Parents Group (1996). Personal communication. 53 Bowmore Road, Noble Park, Vic., Australia.

Attwood, T. (1992) 'Managing the unusual behaviour of children and adults with autism.' *Communication 26*, National Autistic Society, London.

Attwood, T. (1998) *Asperger's Syndrome: A Guide for Parents and Professionals.* London: Jessica Kingsley Publishers.

Attwood, T. (1999) 'Asperger's Syndrome.' Paper presented to seminar group. Asperger Syndrome Parents Support Group, Mt. Waverely Community Centre, Victoria.

Attwood, T. (2000) 'Recent advances in our understanding of Asperger's Syndrome.' Paper presented at Autism Europe Congress 2000, Glasgow.

Baron-Cohen, S. (1989) 'The autistic child's theory of mind: A case of specific developmental delay.' *Journal of Child Psychology and Psychiatry 30*, 285–297.

Baron-Cohen, S., Joliffe, T., Mortimore, C. and Robertson, M. (1997) 'Another advanced test for theory of mind: Evidence from very high functioning adults with autism or Asperger's Syndrome.' *Journal of Child Psychology and Psychiatry 38*, 813–822.

Baron-Cohen, S., Leslie, A.M. and Frith, U. (1985) 'Does the autistic child have a theory of mind?' *Cognition 21*, 37–46.

Bartak, L. (1994). 'Briefing notes on autism and Asperger's Syndrome.' National Association for Autism, Australia.

Bates, E.M. (1977) 'Developing models of mental illness.' In M. Bates (ed) *Models of Madness*. St. Lucia, Queensland: University of Queensland Press.

Beresford, B.A. (1994) 'Resources and strategies: How parents cope with the care of a disabled child.' *Journal of Child Psychiatry 35*, 1, 171–209.

Bitsika, V. (1999) 'Lack of control as a precursor for behavioural problems with people with ASD.' Paper presented at the Autism Australia Conference, Hobart.

Bitsika, V. (2000) 'Understanding and working with autism spectrum disorder.' Disability Services Training Day, Human Services, Melbourne.

Blackman, L. (1999) *Lucy's Story: Autism & Other Adventures*. Brisbane: Book In Hand.

Blagg, N. (1987) *School Phobia and Its Treatment*. Sydney, NSW: Croom Helm.

Blytheway, B. (1995) *Ageism*. Buckingham: Open University Press.

Boyd, G. (1992) 'Family functioning and stress in mothers and children with autism and pervasive development disorders.' *Autism: The Puzzle. Are the Pieces Starting to Fit?* National Conference Proceedings. Glen Iris, Victoria: Autism Victoria

Briggs, F. and Fitzpatrick, C.A. (1994) 'When parents cannot provide care for their children.' In F. Briggs (ed) *Children and Families: An Australian Perspective*. Sydney: Allen and Unwin.

Brill, M.T. (1994) *Keys to Parenting the Child With Autism*. Barron's Education Series. New York: Barron's.

Brinker, R.P., Seifer, R. and Sameroff, A.J. (1994) 'Relations among maternal stress, cognitive development, and early intervention in middle- and low-SES infants with developmental disabilities.' *American Journal on Mental Retardation 98*, 463–480.

Bristol, M.N. and Schopler, E. (1983) 'Stress and coping in families of autistic adolescents.' In E. Schopler and G.B. Mesibov (eds) *Autism in Adolescents and Adults*. New York: Plenum Press.

Bryson, S.E., Wainwright-Sharp, A. and Smith, I.M. (1990) 'Autism: A developmental spatial neglect syndrome?' In J. Enns (ed) *The Development of Attention: Research and Theory*. North Holland: Elsevier.

Burke, K.M. and Richdale, A. (1997) 'Study concerning needs of families and children with a diagnosis of autism, Asperger's Syndrome or

Pervasive Developmental Disorder Not Other Wise Specified.' Royal Melbourne Institute of Technology, Bundoora Campus (unpublished study).

Butera, G. and Haywood, H.C. (1992). 'A cognitive approach to the education of young children with autism.' *Focus on Autistic Behaviour 6*, 6.

Cesaroni, L. and Garber, M. (1991). 'Exploring the experience of autism through firsthand accounts.' *Journal of Autism and Developmental Disorders 21*, 303–313.

Clinebell, H. (1991) *Basic Types of Pastoral Care and Counselling.* London: SCM Press.

Dawson, G. and Lewy, A. (1989) 'Reciprocal subcortical-cortical influences in autism.' In G. Dawson (ed) *Autism: Nature, Diagnosis and Treatment.* New York: Guilford.

De Meyer, M. (1979) *Parents and Children in Autism.* New York: Wiley.

Dunst, C.J., Trivette, C.M. and Deal, A.G. (1988) *Enabling and Empowering Families: Principles and Guidelines for Practice.* Cambridge, MA: Brookline Books.

Dyson, L.L. (1993) 'Response to the presence of a child with disabilities: Parental stress and family functioning over time.' *American Journal of Mental Retardation 98*, 207–218.

Eisenmajer, R. (1996) Conference proceedings from Autism Victoria Conference, Monash Medical Centre, Clayton, Vic. Australia.

Eisenmajer, R. and Prior, M. (1991) 'Cognitive linguistic correlates of 'theory of mind' ability in autistic children.' *British Journal of Developmental Psychology 9*, 351–364.

Engels, G.I., Garnefski, N. and Diekstra, R.E.W. (1993) 'Efficacy of Rational-Emotive therapy: A Quantitative Analysis.' *Journal of Consulting and Clinical Psychology 61*, 1083–1090.

Erbrederis, C. (1997) 'Social work in mental health services.' Community Health II coursebook, fourth year Social Work, Distance Education, Monash University.

Foxx, R.M. (1982) *Decreasing Behaviours of Severely Retarded and Autistic Persons.* Illinois: Research Press.

Foy, E. (1997) 'Parental grieving of childhood disability: A rural perspective.' *Australian Social Work 50*, 39–44.

Frith, U. (1992) *Autism and Asperger Syndrome.* Cambridge: Cambridge University Press.

Ghaziuddin, M. (2000) 'Autism and associated conditions across the life span.' *Autism Conference Proceedings,* Wellington, New Zealand. Wellington: Autistic Association of New Zealand.

Gillberg, C. (1991) 'Clinical and neurobiological aspects of Asperger Syndrome in six family studies.' In U. Frith (ed) *Autism and Asperger Syndrome.* Cambridge: Cambridge University Press.

Gillberg, C. (1999) 'Autism and its spectrum disorders: recent developments.' Paper presented to the Autism Australia Conference, Hobart.

Gillberg, C. and Coleman, M. (1992) *The Biology of the Autistic Syndrome.* (2nd ed.) London: Mac Keith Press.

Gleitman, H. (1991) *Psychology.* (3rd ed.) New York: Norton & Company.

Grandin T. (1995) *Thinking in Pictures and Other Reports from My Life with Autism.* New York: Doubleday.

Grandin, T. and Scariano, M. (1986) *Emergence: Labelled Autistic.* Tunbridge Wells: Costello.

Graves, P. and Bartak, L. (1999) 'Coexistence of disorder of attention and disorders of the autism spectrum.' Paper presented at the Autism Australia Conference, Hobart.

Gray, C. (2000) 'Teaching social understanding with social stories and comic strip conversations.' Jenison, MI: The Gray Center For Learning and Understanding.

Green, J. and Shellenberger, R. (1991) *The Dynamics of Health and Wellness.* USA: Dryder Press.

Grossman, J.B., Klin, A., Carter, A.S. and Volkmar, F.R. (2000) 'Verbal bias in recognition of facial emotions in children with Asperger Syndrome.' *Journal of Child Psychology 41,* 369–379.

Happé, F. (1994) *Autism: An Introduction to Psychological Theory.* London: UCL Press. (Reprinted 1998; all page references are for 1998 edition.)

Happé, F. (1999) 'Central coherence.' Presentation given on 10 November at Australian Technology Park, Sydney. Autism Association of New South Wales.

Harchik, A.E., Harchik, A.J., Luce, S.C. and Jordan, R. (1992) 'The special educational needs of children with Asperger Syndrome.' Educational

Research Into Autism Group, University of Hertfordshire. Paper given at Wakehurst Study Weekend on Asperger Syndrome, Chester, UK.

Harchik, A.E., Harchik, A.J., Luce, S.C. and Sherman, J.A. (1990) 'Teaching autistic and severely handicapped children to recruit praise: Acquisition and generalization.' *Research in Developmental Disabilities II*, 77–95.

Harris V.S. and McHale, S.M. (1989) 'Family life problems, daily care taking activities, and the psychological well-being of mothers of mentally retarded children.' *American Journal of Mental Retardation 94*, 231–239.

Herbert, M. (1990) *Psychology for Social Workers*. Guildford: The British Psychological Society and Macmillan.

Holroyd, J. and McArthur, D. (1976) 'Mental retardation and stress on the parents: A contrast between Down's syndrome and childhood autism.' *American Journal of Mental Deficiency 80*, 431–436.

Janzen, J. (1996) *Understanding the Nature of Autism: A Practical Guide.* Texas: Therapy Skill Builders.

Jefferys, M. (1990) *Growing Old in the Twentieth Century.* London: Routledge.

Kanner, L. (1943) 'Autistic disturbances of affective contact.' *Nervous Child 2*, 217–250.

Kaplan, R.M. and Saccuzzo, D.P. (1997) *Psychological Testing: Principles, Applications and Issues.* (4th ed) Pacific Grove, CA: International Thomson Publishing.

Kellerman, H. and Burry, A. (1991) *Handbook of Psychodiagnostic Testing.* New York, NY: Prentice Hall.

Kennedy, E. and Charles, S.C. (1994) *On Becoming a Counsellor.* Blackburn, Victoria: Collins Dove.

Koegel, R.L., Koegel, L.K. and Surratt, A. (1992) 'Language intervention and disruptive behaviour in preschool children with autism.' *Journal of Autism and Developmental Disorders 22*, 141–151.

Koegel, R.L., Rincincover, A. and Egel, A.L. (1982) *Educating and Understanding Autistic Children.* San Diego, CA: College-Hill Press.

Koegel, R. Schreibman, L., Loos L., Dirlich-Welhelm, H., Funlap, G., Robbins, F. and Plienis, A. (1992) 'Consistent stress profiles in mothers of children with autism.' *Journal of Autism and Developmental Disorders 22*, 205–216.

Kohen-Raz, R., Volkmar, F.R. and Cohen, D.J. (1992) 'Postural control in children with autism.' *Journal of Autism and Developmental Disorders 22*, 427–432.

Lawson, W. (1997). 'Personal insights into Asperger Syndrome.' Paper presented at the National Autism Conference, Monash University, Clayton, Victoria.

Lawson, W. (1998a). *Hope for the future* (level 1). Autism Spectrum Disorder Training Program. Warrnambool, Victoria: Focus For Life.

Lawson, W. (1998b) *Life Behind Glass: A Personal Account of Autism Spectrum Disorder.* Lismore, NSW: Southern Cross University Press.

Lawson, W. (1998c) 'My life as an exchange student with Asperger Syndrome on an exchange programme from Monash University, Australia to The University of Bradford, England.' *Autism: The International Journal of Research and Practice 2*, 290–295.

Lawson, W. (1999a) 'Keys to understanding autism spectrum disorder.' Paper presented at the Autism Australia Conference, Hobart.

Lawson, W. (1999b) *The Rationale and Development of 'Hope For The Future': A Training Program Exploring Autism Spectrum Disorder.* Honours thesis, Dept. of Social Work & Human Services, Monash University, Clayton, Victoria, Australia.

Lovas, I. (1987) 'Behavioural treatment and normal education and intellectual functioning in autistic children.' *Journal of Consulting and Clinical Psychology vol. 55, 1*, 3–9.

Maurice, C. (ed) (1996) *Behavioural Intervention for Young Children with Autism.* Texas: Pro-ed.

Mohammad, G. (2000) 'Depression in persons with autism: diagnosis and treatment.' Conference proceedings, Autistic Association of New Zealand. Wellington, New Zealand.

Mohr, C. and Sharpley, C.F., (1985) 'Elimination of self-injurious behaviour in an autistic child by use of overcorrection.' *Behaviour Change 2*, 143–148. Publication of the Australian Behaviour Modification Association.

Moreno, S. (2000) Personal communication. In association with Maap, PO BOX 524, Crown Point, IN 46308, USA. Email. chart@netnitco.net

Murray, D.K.C. (1992) 'Attention tunnelling and autism.' In P. Shattock and G. Linfoot (eds) *Living with Autism: The Individual, the Family, and the Professional.* Sunderland: Autism Research Unit, University of Sunderland.

Murray, D.K.C. (1995) 'An autistic friendship.' *Psychological Perspectives in Autism 183–193.* Paper originally presented at the Durham conference. In collected papers of Durham proceedings, obtainable from the Autism Research Unit, University of Sunderland, SR2 7EE, or from the National Autistic Society, 393 City Road, London EC1V 1NG.

Murray, D.K.C. (1996) 'Shared attention and speech in autism.' Paper presented at the Durham Conference.

Murray, D.K.C. (1997) 'Normal and otherwise: Living and learning with autism.' Paper presented at the Durham Conference, Durham, UK.

Murray, D.K.C. (2000) 'Autism and computing.' http://www.shifth.mistral.co.uk/autism/index.htm

O'Connor, I., Wilson, J. and Thomas, K. (1991) *Social Work and Welfare Practice.* Melbourne: Longman Cheshire.

Ozonoff, S. and Miller, J.N. (1995) 'Teaching theory of mind: A new approach to social skills training for individuals with autism.' *Journal of Autism and Developmental Disorders 25,* 415–433.

Pain, B. (1990) *Choices and Elderly People: Principles for Social Care and Health Care.* Birmingham: British Association of Social Workers.

Park, C.C. (1983) 'Growing out of autism.' In E. Schopler and G. Mesibov (eds) *Growing out of Autism: The Effects of Autism on the Family.* New York: Plenum Press.

Payne, J. (1996) *All in the Mind.* Oxford: Oxford University Press.

Piaget, J. (1954) *The Construction of Reality in a Child.* New York: Basic Books.

Picker, M., Poling, A. and Parker, A. (1997) 'A review of children's self-injurious behaviour.' *The Psychological Record 29,* 435–452.

Powell, S.D. and Jordan, R.R. (1992) 'Remediating the thinking of pupils with autism: Principles into practice.' *Journal of Autism and Developmental Disorders 22,* 413–418.

Powell, S.D. and Jordan, R.R. (eds) (1997) *Autism and Learning.* London: David Fulton.

Pringle, N.N. and Thompson, P.J. (1986) 'Psychiatric illness: Neuroses, psychoses.' In N.N. Pringle and P.J. Thompson (eds) *Social Work Psychiatry and the Law.* London: William Heinemann Medical Books.

Prior, M. (1992) 'Recent advances in the neuro-psychology of autism.' *Autism: The Puzzle. Are the Pieces Starting to Fit?* National Conference Proceedings. Glen Iris, Victoria: Autism Victoria.

Prior, M. (1998) Keynote address. 'Piecing It Together' Conference, Altona: Western Autistic School, Niddrie, Victoria.

Prior, M. and Hoffmann, W. (1990) 'Brief report: Neuropsychological testing of autistic children through an exploration of frontal lobe tests.' *Journal of Autism and Developmental Disorders 20*, 581–590.

Quill, K., Gurry, S. and Larkin, A. (1989) 'Daily life therapy: A Japanese model for educating children with autism.' *Journal of Autism and Developmental Disorders vol. 19 no.4*, 625–635.

Rankin, K. (1992) 'Escaper.' Family section, *Communication 26*, 2.

Reber, S. (1995) *Dictionary of Psychology* (2nd ed.) London: Penguin Books.

Reed, S.K. (1996) *Cognition.* (4th ed.) Pacific Grove, CA: Brooks/Cole Publishing.

Richdale A.L. and Prior M.R. (1992) 'Urinary cortisol circadian rhythm in a group of high-functioning children with autism.' *Journal of Autism and Developmental Disorders 22*, 433–542.

Rickarby, G., Carruthers, A. and Mitchell, M. (1991) 'Brief report: Biological factors associated with Asperger Syndrome.' *Journal of Autism and Developmental Disorders 21*, 341–392.

Rimland, B. (1993) 'Developmental disorders: The autism continuum.' *Journal of Autism and Developmental Disorders 4*, 71–85.

Rutter, M. (1983) 'Cognitive deficits in the pathogenesis of autism.' *Journal of Child Psychology and Psychiatry 24*, 513–531.

Rutter, M. and Schopler, E. (1978) *Autism: A Reappraisal of Concepts and Treatment.* New York: Plenum Press.

Santrock, J.W. (1989) *Lifespan Development.* (3rd ed.) Dubuque, Iowa: University of Texas and Wm. C. Brown.

Schopler, E. (1995) *Parent Survival Manual: A Guide to Crisis Resolution in Autism.* New York: Plenum Press.

Schopler, E. and Mesibov, G.B. (1983) *Growing out of Autism: The Effects of Autism on the Family.* New York: Plenum Press.

Scottish Society for Autism (2000) Personal Communication. CETA, Hilton House, Alloa business park, Alloa, FK10 3SA.

Sharpe, P. and Ross, S. (1987) *Living Psychology.* Brunswick, Victoria: Scribe Publications.

Sharpley, C. and Bitsika, V. (1999) 'Conducting support groups which meet the specific needs of parents with ASD children.' Paper presented at the Autism Australia Conference, Hobart.

Sharpley, C., Bitsika,V., and Efremidis, B. (1997) 'The influence of gender, parental health, and perceived expertise of assistance upon the well-being of parents of children with autism.' *Journal of Intellectual & Developmental Disability 22*, 19–28.

Shattock, P. (1990) 'Some implications of basic psysilogical research for the behaviour and treatment of people with autism.' Conference proceedings, from 'Experimental Psychology and the Autistic Syndromes.' Durham, National Autistic Society, 257–285.

Shattock, P. and Savery, D. (1997) 'Perspectives from the individual, the family and the professional.' *Living and Learning with Autism* Conference Proceedings. Sunderland: Autism Research Unit, University of Sunderland. Website: *http://osiris.sunderland.ac.uk/autism/shattock*

Stokes, T.F. and Baer, D.M. (1977) 'An implicit technology of generalisation.' *Journal of Applied Behaviour Analysis 10*, 349–367.

Sullivan, K., Zaitchik, D. and Tager-Flusberg, H. (1994) 'Preschoolers can attribute second-order beliefs.' *Developmental Psychology 30*, 395–402.

Tantam, D. (1988) 'Asperger's Syndrome or schizoid personality disorder?' *British Journal of Psychiatry 153*, 783–791.

Tantam, D., Holmes D. and Cordess C. (1993) 'Nonverbal expression in autism of Asperger type.' *Journal of Autism and Developmental Disorders 23*, 111–134.

Tonge, B.J., Dissanayake, C. and Brereton, A.V. (1994) 'Autism: Fifty years on from Kanner.' *Journal of Pediatric Child Health 30*, 102–107.

VicHealth (1996) *Adolescent Health Fact Sheet.* The Child Health Information Centre, Royal Children's Hospital, Parkville, Victoria.

Wainwright-Sharp, J.A. and Bryson, S.E. (1993) 'Visual orienting deficits in high-functioning people with autism.' *Journal of Autism and Developmental Disorders 23*, 1–13.

Walker, A.J. (1997) 'Separate realities; a plain narrative of a posteriori cognition: An analogue for comparisons with and between Asperger syndrome and other autistic spectrum conditions.' *Living and Learning with Autism* Conference Proceedings. Sunderland: Autism Research Unit, University of Sunderland.

Williams, D. (1994) *Somebody Somewhere.* Moorebank, NSW: Transworld.

Wing, L. (1981) 'Asperger's syndrome: A clinical account.' *Psychological Medicine 11*, 115–129.

Wing, L. and Attwood, A. (1987) 'Syndromes of autism and a typical development.' In D.J. Cohen, A. Donnellan and R. Paul (eds) *Handbook of Autism and Pervasive Developmental Disorders.* New York: Wiley.

Suggested Reading List

General Reference

Attwood, T. (1998) *Asperger's Syndrome: A Guide for Parents and Professionals.* London: Jessica Kingsley Publishers.

Baron-Cohen, S., and Bolton, P. (1993) *Autism: The Facts.* Oxford University Press.

Frith, U. (1989) *Autism: Explaining the Enigma.* Oxford: Basil Blackwell.

Frith, U. (ed) (1991) *Autism and Asperger Syndrome.* Cambridge: Cambridge University Press.

Gillingham, G. (1995) *Autism: Handle with Care.* Texas: Future Education Inc.

Howlin, P. (1997) *Autism: Preparing for Adulthood.* London: Routledge.

Howlin, P. (1998) *Children with Autism and Asperger Syndrome: A Guide for Practitioners and Carers.* London: John Wiley & Sons Ltd.

Siegel, B. (1996). *The World of the Autistic Child.* New York: Oxford University Press.

Wing, L. (1996) *The Autistic Spectrum: A Guide for Parents and Professionals.* London: Constable.

Text Books

Gillberg, C., and Coleman, M. (1992) *The Biology of the Autistic Syndromes.* (2nd edition) London: Mac Keith Press.

Happé, F. (1994) *Autism: An Introduction to Psychological Theory.* London: UCL Press.

Jordan, R.R. (1999) *Autistic Spectrum Disorders – An Introductory Handbook for Practitioners.* London: David Fulton.

Ratey, J.J. and Johnson, C. (1997) *Shadow Syndromes.* Pantheon.

Schopler, E., and Mesibov, G.B. (1992) *High-Functioning Individuals with Autism.* New York: Plenum Press.

Training Programs and approaches

Fullerton, A. Stratton, J. Coyne, P. and Gray, C. (eds) (1996) *Higher Functioning Adolescents and Young Adults with Autism: A Teachers Guide.* (Illustrated by Georgianne Thomas) Monterrey: Pro-Ed.

Gray, C. (1993) *Original Social Stories.* Arlington, TX: Future Horizons

Gray, C. (1994) *Comic strip conversations.* Arlington, TX: Future Horizons.

Janzen, J. (1996). *Understanding the Nature of Autism: A Practical Guide.* Texas: Therapy Skill Builders.

Koegel, R., and Koegel, L. (1995) *Teaching Children with Autism.* Baltimore, MD: Brookes.

Lawson, W. (1998) *'Hope For The Future' (Workshop).* Focus For Life, 4 Foster Street, Warrnambool, Vic., Australia.

Maurice, C. (ed) (1996) *Behavioural Intervention for Young Children with Autism.* Texas: Pro-ed.

McClannahan, L.E. and Krantz, P.J. (1999) *Activity Schedules for Children with Autism.* Princeton, NJ: The Princeton Child Development Institute.

National Autistic Society, (1997) *Approaches to Autism.* London: National Autistic Society.

Smith, M.D., Belcher, R.G. and Juhrs, P. (1994) *A Guide to Successful Employment for Individuals with Autism.* Baltimore, MD: Paul Brookes.

Parents and Families

Brill, M.T. (1994). *Keys to Parenting the Child with Autism.* New York: Barron's Education Series.

Davies, J. (1994) *Children with Autism: A Booklet for Brothers and Sisters.* Nottingham: The Early Diagnosis Centre.

Harris, S.L. (1994) *Siblings of Children with Autism. A Guide for Families.* Bethesda, MD: Woodbine House.

Jordan, R. and Powell, S. (1995) *Understanding and Teaching Children with Autism.* Chichester: John Wiley Sons Ltd.

Jordan, R. and Jones, G. (1999) *Meeting the Needs of Children with Autistic Spectrum Disorders.* London: David Fulton Publishers.

Lewis, L. (1999) *Special Diets for Special Kids. Understanding and Implementing Special Diets to Aid in the Treatment of Autism and Related Developmental Disorders.* Arlington, TX: Future Horizons Inc.

Maurice, E. (1993) *Let Me Hear Your Voice.* New York: Ballantine Books.

Morgan, H. (1996) *Adults with Autism: A Guide to Theory and Practice.* Cambridge: Cambridge University Press

Powell, S. and Jordan, R. (eds) (1997) *Autism and Learning: A Guide to Good Practice.* London: David Fulton Publishers.

Powers, M.D. (1989) *Children with Autism: A Parents Guide.* London: Woodbine House.

Schopler, E. (1995) *Parent Survival Manual: A Guide to Crisis Resolution in Autism.* New York: Plenum Press.

Autobiographical Accounts

Barron, J., and Barron, S. (1992) *There's A Boy in Here.* New York: Simon & Schuster.

Blackman, L. (1999). *Lucy's Story: Autism and Other Adventures.* Queensland, Australia: Book in hand.

Gerland, G. (1997). *A Real Person: Life on the Outside.* London: Souvenir Press Ltd.

Grandin, T. (1996) *Emergence: Labelled Autistic.* New York, NY: Warner.

Grandin, T. (1996) *Thinking in Pictures.* New York, NY: Vintage Books.

Holliday Willey, L. (1999) *Pretending to be Normal.* London: Jessica Kingsley Publishers.

Lawson, W. (1998) *Life Behind Glass.* Lismore, NSW: Southern Cross University Press and (2000) London: Jessica Kingsley Publishers.

Williams, D. (1992) *Nobody Nowhere.* London: Jessica Kingsley Publishers.

Williams, D. (1994) *Somebody Somewhere.* London: Jessica Kingsley Publishers.

Subject Index

Author Index